Filipino Fighting Arts

FILIPINO FIGHTING ARTS

Theory and Practice

Mark V. Wiley

Unique Publications
4201 Vanowen Place
Burbank, California 91505

Disclaimer

Please note that the author and publisher of this book are NOT RESPONSIBLE in any manner whatsoever for any injury that may result from practicing the techniques and/or following the instructions given within. Since the physical activities described herein may be too strenuous in nature for some readers to engage in safely, it is essential that a physician be consulted prior to training.

For Jeraldine and Alexander

Contents

The Filipino Fighting Arts

Foreword

by Reynaldo S. Galang,
Bakbakan International
Makati City, Philippines

Mark V. Wiley has once again enriched the world of martial arts with his latest book, *Filipino Fighting Arts: Theory and Practice*. Driven by a mission and vision that manifests his love for the Philippine combat arts, Mark's research and writing faithfully espouse the very soul of the warrior arts of the Philippines.

The various styles of the Philippine fighting arts universally emphasize the values and virtues of the endless search for knowledge *(karunungan)*, of unwavering loyalty and dedication *(katapatan)*, and of absolute justice or truth *(katarungan)*.

This book epitomizes this single-minded pursuit of knowledge that can only be quenched by keeping an open and discerning mind. Mark generously shares with us his dedication and passion for the fighting arts. This book enables the reader to partake of the wealth of knowledge that is abundant in the Filipino martial arts. Despite the seemingly overt individual characteristics of each style, dedicated study and extensive experience will reveal the unavoidable functional similarity of these arts. True and realistic fighting arts, regardless of origin or ancestry, share the absolute and finite truth of effectiveness and simplicity in combat.

Mark's extensive research into and coverage of the Philippine weapon arts—the popular as well as the obscure—does much to clarify and preserve the individual concepts and philosophies that make each unique while at the same time alike.

In essence, Mark V. Wiley has again compiled and written a priceless reference work on the Filipino martial arts that will be treasured by generations of martial artists and is destined to become a classic.

Foreword

by Antonio E. Somera,
Bahala Na Association
Stockton, California, USA

It is indeed my honor and privilege to write this forward for Mark V. Wiley's latest book, *Filipino Fighting Arts: Theory and Practice.*

Not too many years ago, the Filipino martial arts were so closed and non-commercial that many people did not know of their existence. In some cases, our own Filipino decadences did not know that the Philippines had its own truly effective and meticulous self-defense art. And it was not until World War II that the American public came to know the Filipinos as an educated people with their own expertise in Jungle warfare.

Many of our Filipino forefathers used their martial skills to protect their families against the atrocities of war. During World War II, many of our Filipino family members had volunteered to return to the Philippines to protect our homeland. Under the command of General Douglas MacArthur these young men engaged in secret and dangerous military missions to help recapture the Philippine Islands from the Japanese. These young fighting men of the First and Second Filipino Battalions became some of the most decorated solders in the Asian theater of war. At the end of World War II, many of our experts in Filipino martial arts retired into civilian life. During the next thirty years their dreams of raising families was their most important agenda—not promoting their ancestral fighting arts.

Thus, it was not until the late sixties that the Filipino martial arts of Escrima and Arnis came into the public eye, through the pioneering efforts of people like Dan Inosanto,

Richard Bustillo, and Lucky Lucaylucay. Their efforts were so overwhelming that many practitioners of these arts attempted to follow in their foot steps and carry on their mission of helping the public better understand the Filipino martial arts.

Over the past decade, Mark V. Wiley has dedicated his time and energies in the propagation of the Filipino martial arts. From his countless hours of training with the many masters and grandmasters of the arts, his numerous travels across the United States and to the Philippines, and his tiring and meticulous research, Mr. Wiley has made every attempt to share his personal experience and research with those that would endure his timeless efforts. Much of his research came out of his own curiosity to discover first hand what these arts are truly about. And he has indeed given us all a greater and more in-depth awareness of our rich and beautiful cultural heritage with his body of written work. His selfless efforts are highly commended.

This current book is the most in-depth and well-documented work on the individual Filipino weapon-based systems. While many people think all Filipino arts are merely "stick fighting," and their techniques and training are the same, this book shows us otherwise. Although there are too many Filipino martial arts to include in one text, this book offers perhaps the best representation available on the two-dozen or so arts it does include. The reader can't help but further his knowledge and understanding of these arts as a result of this book.

Mark V. Wiley is indeed one of the leading authorities on the Filipino martial arts. Although many people may disagree with his research findings—generally as a result of their own limited views and exposure—I have known Mark to be truthful, honest, and sincere. I truly respect him as a writer, as a practitioner, and as a man. I therefore congratulate him on his selfless efforts in bringing this priceless information to our attention and making it available to the general public. His many years of dedication to the Filipino martial arts have been truly inspiring and we will all continue to benefit from his research and writings.

Foreword

by Krishna K. Godhania,
Institute of Filipino Martial Arts
Warwick, England

There are so few trustworthy publications on the Filipino Arts in the English language that the publication of such a work can only be described as a landmark. Furthermore, when it is produced by so competent a researcher and practitioner as Mark V. Wiley, the occasion is one to be savored.

Filipino Fighting Arts: Theory and Practice is a detailed work, which highlights the concepts and principles that form the essence of any style or system. It is not merely another "how to" book on the martial arts. By expounding on theory and practice, in addition to illustrating specific techniques, the author has given the reader the opportunity to really understand nearly thirty distinct Filipino martial art systems.

Reliable works are rare and so, incidentally, are the men capable of undertaking them. The readers of this book, and I imagine there will be plenty of them, owe a debt of gratitude to Mark V. Wiley. For he has set to all those who come after him a formidable standard. Yet, that is no less than one would expect of him.

Read on and enjoy!

INTRODUCTION

The Filipino fighting arts are so vast and dynamic that isolated works do them no justice. Each article, book, or video has its own specific focus, and therefore generally present the arts in a one-dimensional manner. And so it is necessary that a number of works be written, each with its own focus, as otherwise only thin light will be shed on an otherwise dense subject.

I have previously published two books on the Filipino martial arts. The first was an instructional book on one specific style of Escrima, while the second was a comprehensive overview of the history, culture, and masters of the Filipino arts in general. And while the books are comprehensive, neither is able to deal with every facet of a single art form (as in the first book) or the multitude of arts (as in the second book).

It was with this in mind that I set about writing a book on the Filipino fighting arts that would not rehash the same information found elsewhere, but one that would present a fair and unbiased presentation of the arts from a training, theoretical, and technical fighting perspective—those things that construct the arts, giving them their individual style, characteristics, and effect their fighting techniques.

This book, too, has its focus, as it offers almost nothing in terms of culture and history of the arts or biographies of their masters. However, in an attempt to balance my other writings, this book offers a structured, side-by-side presentation of twenty-seven Filipino fighting arts in terms of categories of training, training methods and progressions, fighting concepts, theories, and strategies, and photographic depiction's of their respective fighting techniques. This book, then, is not so much a dissertation, analysis, or comparison of these dynamic arts, but a comprehensive presentation of Filipino weapon-based systems—some of which have not heretofore been written about.

It is hoped that this book will not only expose and promote the Filipino arts as their respective masters understand and perpetuate them, but that it will inspire the masters to write in-depth books on their individual systems and styles. It is only in this way that the frivolous myths surrounding these arts—such as that their is but one martial art in the Philippines, or that all Filipino arts can be traced to a single "mother" art—will be seen in their true light and put to rest.

It should be noted that the arts presented herein are "Filipino" fighting arts. That is, fighting arts developed by Filipinos (both in the Philippines and abroad). What are not included are the dozens of Filipino-based martial arts that have been developed by Westerners around the world. The book also only presents Filipino weapon-based systems, and not the vast number of Philippine empty hand arts. These are subjects best left for other studies and publications.

The reader will notice that some chapters are longer and more in depth than others. While I tried in earnest to give equal depth and page length to each art, at times it was nearly impossible as a result of several issues. First, some systems are just more extensive and comprehensive than others. This is not an indication that one art is necessarily more combative than another, but more an indication of system specialization and depth of curriculum. Second, many masters of these arts simply do not think of their arts in terms of concepts, theories, principles, strategies, or training progressions. As a result, they are unable to articulate the hows and whys of their methods in these terms. But this does not reflect on their skills, as their systems are pragmatic fighting arts based on intuition and practical experience—and not necessarily intellectualism. Third, some masters, while amenable to being featured in this book, were leery to share their "secrets" with the public.

As with all of my writings, I only include here arts that I have either personally studied or where I personally met with a master of the system to interview him directly, observe his style, and experience his movements first hand. As a result, I do not present secondary or tertiary information based on what others have previously written. It is only by doing proper research and going to the source that the perpetuation of misinformation so vast and prevalent in this field can be limited and eventually eliminated. With this in mind, any and all mistakes found herein are my own. I thus apologize in advance to the masters and practitioners of these arts if I have in any way offended them by my errors.

Moreover, while comprehensive, this book is not complete, as there are far too many Filipino fighting arts for one person to possibly research or one book to expect to cover. I thus apologize to the dozens of other masters I did interview and/or study with, whose arts do not appear in this volume. However, given space limitations and wishing to expose as many systems as possible, many arts that appear in my other writings do not appear here, thus leaving room for other, less-well-known arts.

This book was not written in a vacuum, but with the gracious assistance and support of a number of people. I extend my deepest appreciation and gratitude to the following individuals: Alejandro Abrian, Carlos Aldrete-Phan, J. Christoph Amberger, Tom Arroyo, Sam Babikian, Abondio Baet, Gregorio Baet, John Bain, Alfredo Bandalan, Ron Beaubien, Tom Bisio,

Joe Breidenstein, Angel Cabales, Dionisio Cañete, Robert Chu, Alexander Co, Arnulfo Cuesta, Omichael delRosario, Travis DeVitas, Antonio Diego, Tom Dy Tang, Ramiro Estalilla, Frederico Fernandez, Reynaldo S. Galang, Leo M. Giron, Bobby Go King, Krishna K. Godhania, Patrick Gross, Jane Hallander, Miles Henderson, Josh Holzer, Willie Houston, Antonio Ilustrisimo, Graham Jamieson, Felipe Jocano Jr., Jim Johnson, Chris Kent, Mark Komuro, Porferio Lanada, Dr. Jopet Laraya, Eddie Lastra, Rene Latosa, Benjamin Luna Lema, Amante Mariñas, Rolly Maximo, Jose Mena, Rick Mitchell, Sonny Napial, Carlos Navarro, Rene Navarro, Ngo Vinh-Hoi, Alex Ngoi, Arnold Noche, Rafael Pambuan, Abner Pasa, Dr. Marieno Pizarro, Ernesto Presas, Remy Presas, Christopher Ricketts, Baltizar Z. Sayoc, Christopher C. Sayoc, Sr., Chris Sayoc, Jr., Jimmie Sayoc, Antonio E. Somera, Edgar G. Sulite, Bobby Taboada, Steve Tarani, Jerson Tortal, Pacito Velez, Curtis Wong, Woody Woodman, Elmer Ybañez, and Miguel Zubiri.

—Mark V. Wiley
Bel Air, Maryland

THE
FILIPINO
FIGHTING
ARTS

Master Frederico Fernandez

1

ARNIS DEFENSE SILAT

After studying Modern Arnis under Remy Presas, classical Arnis under Florencio Pasqual, and Indonesian Kamojak Silat under Claro Siaco, at the age of forty Frederico Fernandez developed a style he calls Arnis Defense Silat. Fernandez officially began teaching this style in 1994 while working as a graphic artist in Alcubar, Saudi Arabia. Fernandez again resides in Manila, where he teaches and continues to develop his fighting art.

Training Progressions

As an easy-to-learn and simplified self-defense system, Arnis Defense Silat focuses on the use of the empty hands and the single stick. As this system is a combined Filipino and Indonesian art, it does not follow the general progression of learning weapon skills prior to the empty hands, as do many Filipino styles. In this art students are first introduced to the empty hand aspects of Silat and Arnis, after which they are taught the fundamental single stick methods of Arnis.

Regarding the empty hand dimension, students are first taught how to stand, how to move in their stances, and then how to apply their techniques while assuming various postures. Once this is learned, the techniques of the style are taught in a progressive manner, beginning with paralyzing techniques, then knock-out techniques, followed by breaking techniques, and then killing techniques.

The focus of Arnis Defense Silat is on holding and releasing techniques. The rationale being that if you are only versed in stick fighting and are grabbed by an opponent, you will be at a loss and thus defeated. The more releasing techniques learned, the less the possibility that someone will be able to lock your limbs or pin you down. Moreover, practitioners of this art believe that even given a sudden attack, regardless of type, techniques of holding and releasing can easily be applied without hesitation.

When learning holding and releasing techniques, students are first taught how to control the attacker, beginning with how to release from wrist grabs. There are twenty-five techniques performed from each arm—both parallel and cross—totaling one-hundred releasing techniques in all.

Striking is also used in conjunction with releasing, especially if the attacker is holding too firmly for one to maneuver and release his grip with counter locks of his own. At such times a punch to the face or neck is employed to distract the attacker to then effect a lock release or reversal. However, with dedicated practice of the art's exercises, this is no longer a problem as practitioners are able to respond accordingly without delay, thus preventing the attacker from obtaining a firm hold. Then, if a punch is thrown, the arm can easily be controlled, redirected, and locked.

The dancing or forms of the art are taught next, of which there are two. One dance is prearranged and the other is not. While there is a total of two-hundred movements in the form proper, it is broken down into sets of seven movements—a number believed to be good for self-defense. Students learn each set of seven and then combine them as they like. While beginners are first taught the form in a prearranged, numbered sequence, after they perfect it they must be able to do it on command by section number. The instructor will call out a grouping of numbers, in any sequence, at which

time the student must connect the movements together in the order commanded.

All counter attacks have a preset number and are found within the form. In essence, the art contains two-hundred holding and releasing techniques, a low kick to the groin, and a stomp from the knee to the instep of the foot, various sweeping techniques, scissors takedowns, and a low sidekick to the knee wherein the practitioner first drops low to the ground and then kicks. Open hand techniques consist of holding, releasing, and breaking techniques, a palm heel to the nose, a hammer fist, and an upward vertical elbow strike directed to either the sternum, chin, or nose.

After skill has been gained in the hand-to-hand techniques, students are introduced to stick fighting. In this category are taught both stick against stick and empty hands against stick techniques.

Students first learn to block the stick with their own stick and then how to counterattack. Since a weapons encounter is considered to be "life and death," rather than blocking and countering practitioners of Arnis Defense Silat prefer to lower their body to avoid the strike and smash the hand of the attacker with their weapon. Along these lines, it is believed that if you do not stand low to the ground, the attacker can counter your counter, and you will lose the fight.

Following basic blocks and counters, the Arnis dance is introduced. This form is prearranged and consists of ten techniques. Rather than having a set of "angles of attack," as do most Arnis styles, Arnis Defense Silat's ten strikes come after the opponent's attack. As such, practitioners can execute all ten of their blocks against each of the five, seven, or twelve strikes of most other styles. In this way, it is believed that you are the one manipulating the attacks of your opponent, allowing you to easily strike the attacker. Thus, every time practitioners of this art are attacked, they automatically employ the empty hand and/or stick techniques at the moment of attack initiation, to either the inside or outside of the opponent's attacking limb. This is the concurrent use of Silat and Arnis employed against a single attack.

Training Methods

Training drills in this art are few, but nonetheless essential. One of the most important elements to effectively employing fighting techniques is timing. To develop timing, practitioners of Arnis Defense Silat practice their blocks, joint locks, striking techniques, and counters in every class. Practitioners believe that the best way to develop timing is through mastering the holding-and-releasing and the blocking-and-countering exercises.

These exercises are similar, and set in two parts. The first part finds one partner striking and the other blocking and countering. The second part finds one partner striking, the other blocking and countering, and then the first partner countering the counter of the second partner. These exercises are done empty hand against empty hand (employing strikes, holds, and releases), empty hand against weapon (employing parries, strikes, holds, and disarms), and weapon against weapon (employing direct hits, blocks, strikes, and disarms).

Fighting Strategies

The key strategy of Arnis Defense Silat is how to get out of a hold, how to attack, and how to block in such a way that an opponent can not strike you back. To apply this strategy, practitioners either move to the back or to the side of the opponent the moment an attack is initiated.

When employing the holding and releasing techniques, it is important not to step back. Once a limb is grabbed you can maneuver it to block a second strike, also locking that limb in the process. This is the method of controlling the attacker, after which breaking techniques are employed. Breaking techniques are essential to the style, for they end a fight quickly by breaking the attacker's bone and sending him into shock. Moreover, by employing the strategy of controlling the attacker's limb, one does not have to see the opponent to know where he will strike next, as his intentions can be felt.

There are only two defensive entering movements in Arnis Defense Silat: moving to the inside and to the outside of the attacker's limbs. When going in, the left hand is held at the right shoulder. In this way, if the opponent attempts to counter, his strike can be deflected or intercepted and his limbs automatically locked. In essence, immediately after blocking the strike, exponents of this style move in and hit the hand, grab, lock, strike, and then break the attacking or defending limb.

Practitioners of Arnis Defense Silat also advocate that one must never employ a technique that is too complicated. The rationale being that if one has memorized too many counters against as many techniques, they will be confused when the time comes to employ them in an altercation. So, it is best to be simple in thought and action.

Another strategy is to try and discern what type of attack an opponent will use. For example, a boxer employs both of his hands in combination, so if you are looking at one of his hands, he may hit you with the other. However, if you are expecting him to hit you with either hand, you can counter his attack. And if you want to neutralize his hands upon making contact with them, you must parry the lead hand first.

Even if it is being used as a fake to set up a follow-up strike, parry it anyway and then move to his outside. Here you are in the better position.

This idea leads into the other concepts and strategies employed in Arnis Defense Silat. These include: parrying and striking simultaneously; striking low when the attacker strikes high; striking high when the attackers strikes low; baiting the opponent to entangle his arms; immediately dropping to the ground and kicking the attacker's legs to cripple him from the onset; and, when ground fighting, using one leg as bait and the other for the actual strike or sweep.

Free-Sparring

There is no empty hand or weapon free-sparring practice in Arnis Defense Silat, as practitioners consider this to be too dangerous. Moreover, since neither Silat nor Arnis are considered sport—at least not by practitioners of this art—and the techniques are learned in a realistic and spontaneous manner, if sparring were attempted, after the first strike was thrown it would be over as the other person would respond automatically and with full force, perhaps blinding or otherwise accidentally injuring his sparring partner.

Master Rey Galang

2

BAKBAKAN KALI

Bakbakan Kali has recently come into its own as an art distinct from its parent art, Kalis Ilustrisimo. While the core techniques of the two systems are similar, Bakbakan Kali encompasses more prearranged forms, drills, and training methods than does its predecessor. And in addition to the core techniques of the Ilustrisimo system, Bakbakan Kali incorporates techniques and training concepts from the arts of Sagasa, Lameco Eskrima, Sinawali, and Placido Yambao's *espada y daga*. These new elements were synthesized into the Bakbakan Kali system by Rey Galang, the international director of the Bakbakan association.

Training Progressions

Training in Bakbakan Kali emphasizes coordination, such that footwork and hand movements are practiced in integrated drills, never separately. All classroom training is done in sections, beginning with stick patterns with basic footwork as a warm-up, moving on to single stick training, then

knife training, followed by coordinated drills, and concluding with *espada y daga* or mixed long- and short-weapon exercises.

Beginners are taught at the same time as advanced practitioners, giving them an idea and overview of the system they are learning. Should the novice show an inability to follow the drills, a senior student or assistant instructor is then assigned to cover their areas of difficulty, separate and apart from the rest of the group. Once they are able to cope with the basics, the beginner is again integrated into the group in the succeeding session, and correspondingly tutored as needed.

All students of Bakbakan Kali are required to know the foundation forms and techniques of their art, and each is required to take turns leading the class as the sessions progress. This practice at once forces and encourages students to perfect their studies to a point where their confidence to perform and their ability to lead a class become routine and expected.

There is no intimidation through rank segregation in Bakbakan Kali, as no overt symbols of rank are worn or displayed by its practitioners. The distinction between beginner, intermediate, and advanced students

is evident in their respective perform-
ances. Individual fighting skills and
performance are stressed and sought
more than any form of ranking.
Furthermore, students wishing to
learn more than they are able to cope
with will find that the true measure
of progress is found in the ability to
apply their learned skills and not in
the gross acquisition of techniques.
Moreover, mere intellectual knowledge of the art is frowned upon, as
such knowledge must also be proven
and applied in actual practice.
Performance during free-sparring sessions, then, is the milestone by which
a practitioner's progress is measured
and judged.

Training Methods

Bakbakan Kali places heavy emphasis
on basics, which are repeated session after session until they
become second nature. While there are numerous prearranged
solo forms, the art contains very few two-person drills, as these
are believed to create false confidence and make one compla-
cent. Instead (and again), a premium is placed on free-sparring.

Training in Bakbakan Kali is always divided into two major
divisions: technical—where drills and techniques are practiced
to perfection—and practical—where one tries to apply their
techniques in full-contact sparring bouts. Thus, each training
session includes training in both technical and practical skills.

While practiced, solo forms are regarded as lesson plans or memory aids. It is the individual components of the forms that are important and thus broken down and rigorously practiced. The forms provide the link or the flow from one technique to another. Techniques, of course, are the basis of the forms.

Multi-drill forms, known as *balangkas,* are introduced early in the training to provide students with a guide to the fundamentals of the system. Students are discouraged from tackling the longer forms, known as *sayaw,* until they can satisfactorily perform the *balangkas.*

Fighting Strategies

There are three primary concepts or fighting strategies employed in Bakbakan Kali. The first is known as *dakip-diwa—* which refers to a combat-oriented mind-set. *Dakip-diwa* implies that one must always be attuned to the demands, opportunities, and evolution of combat. Whether one is fighting in a ring or merely going about their daily routine, his mind-set must be one of awareness but not of stress. *Dakip-diwa* forces one to assess each situation for potential danger and opportunity.

The concept of *prakcion* or "fraction" could be likened to a stop-hit in fencing or fighting in broken rhythm. This allows one to sneak in-between an opponent's natural pacing to disrupt his defensive or offensive actions.

The concept of *enganyo* is the art of feinting or deception and is the third major strategy used in Bakbakan Kali. A study of the many *balangkas* or drills found within the system yields deceptive strategies that dictate the direction of combat that can force an opponent to make mistakes.

It is believed that the above strategies can only be actualized and proven through one true medium: free-sparring. Concepts, attributes, and strategies are mere words. Application is the proof of the pudding.

Free-Sparring

Bakbakan Kali is essentially a sparring-oriented fighting art, wherein sparring is believed to be the ultimate test of acquired skills and the application of techniques and strategies. Even at early stages in training, students are encouraged to participate in free-sparring matches until this becomes the norm rather than the exception.

Novices begin their sparring training with limited-target free-sparring matches. This limited target may take the form of strikes to the weapon-hand and forearm only. Throughout this early and basic form of free-sparring, practitioners are made aware of the opportunities and pitfalls of fighting from both "closed" and "open" guard positions. In addition, the advantages of the system's forward, aggressive stance as opposed to a reversed, defensive stance is also brought to light.

After a period of time, this limited-target free-sparring progresses to open-target free-sparring, where specific target limitations are removed, with the exception of thrusts to the face (unless a proper face mask is worn).

In the early stages of open-target free-sparring students are encouraged to wear as much protective gear as they feel necessary. In the later stages, most of the experienced practitioners limit their protective gear to a groin protector, knee and elbow pads, gloves, and a helmet or fencing mask, allowing them to better understand the pain of the strikes and reality of combat.

Grandmaster Venancio Bacon

3

BALINTAWAK ARNIS

Balintawak Arnis is a straight-forward and hard-hitting stick fighting art. It was developed by Venancio "Anciong" Bacon, who had a background in various Escrima styles, Filipino grappling (Dumog, Combat Judo), and Western boxing. And while Bacon had a sense of "what works," his method of presenting that information to students was often scattershot. It was at the hands of one of his disciples, Atty. Jose Villacin, that the style of Balintawak was formed into a progressive training system. And while there are now currently a number of Balintawak "systems" being propagated around the world—such as those of Bacon, Villacin, Teofilo Velez, Bobby Taboada, Bobby Go King, Ted Buot, and others—they are all based in the same core techniques and concepts.

Training Progressions

While there is no definitive ranking structure used throughout the many branches of Balintawak, a basic structure to training has emerged form the original core material as developed and taught by Bacon. It was the ingenuity of Villasen who systematized the style by categorizing and linking the techniques and methods into so-called "groupings." These "groupings" have made it possible for students to advance within the system in an orderly fashion by progressively developing skills in related techniques.

In general, novices are first introduced to the system's twelve basic strikes—first executed with control and then with full power. The strikes fall along the following sequence: 1) left temple, 2) right temple, 3) right ribs or elbow, 4) left ribs or elbow, 5) stomach thrust, 6) right side of chest, 7) left side of chest, 8) left knee, 9) right knee, 10) right side of face, 11) left side of face, 12) head to solar plexus.

After students memorize the strikes, they learn the appropriate blocks and counters for each. When learning these, the instructor will first strike at the student in the one-to-twelve striking sequence, which the students will block and counter in turn. Striking in sequence allows students to develop the correct muscle memory of each movement. Once the basics are developed the teacher will strike "at random," which develops timing, reflexes, and the ability to react without conscious thought.

It is interesting to note that while practicing these strikes, blocks, and counters, no formal stances are employed. Rather, there is a general fighting stance similar to that used in Western boxing, which finds the practitioner standing with one leg forward, both knees bent, the heel of the back foot raised, with the stick resting on or above the lead shoulder and the left hand held close to the face. It is from this basic "stance" that body shifting, torso twisting, stepping, and evading movements are executed. The short distance between the legs allows for quick advancing and retreating movements and explosive attacks.

This basic foundation is generally followed by the "grouping" techniques, which is a set of five pre-arranged attack and defense sequences that train efficient striking and effective blocking. These "groupings" offer defenses to an opponent's possible blocks and counters of the Balintawak practitioner's strikes. They are especially useful in developing the ability to "flow" continuously from technique to technique, as Balintawak is of the philosophy that an opponent will be able to block and counter at least some of your strikes, thus illustrating the art's realistic view of fighting.

The first group develops skills in blocking, lifting, and clearing an opponent's strike; the second group develops lifting and clearing with head movement; the third group develops preparation for body flexibility; the fourth group develops preparation for speed and reflexes; and the fifth group develops defenses against punches while in stick combat. Each group is first trained in sequence by itself. After a level of skill is attained, the groupings are mixed and matched and performed "at random" at high speeds. This level of practice develops honed reflexes, timing, distancing, and speed.

Once the "groupings" are learned, they become the nucleus or platform of the Balintawak system. From these block and counter drills are added the techniques of butting, pushing, pulling, disarming, and locking. And within this platform are developed skills in direct blocking and countering, blocking with evasive movement, simultaneous attack and defense, body leaning, twisting, ducking, and shifting to accentuate power, movement, and evasiveness.

Training Methods

While there are no pre-arranged solo or two-person forms *per se* in Balintawak Arnis, the training is predominantly carried out in two-person drills. From the onset of training, students engage in "give-and-take" exchanges with a teacher or training partner. It is this emphasis on personal combative effectiveness that gives this art its signature style.

The basic blocks and counters are first trained along the one-to-twelve striking sequence and then "at random." This initial method of learning to defend against a single strike, followed by another single strike, and so on, allows the novice to develop a sense of spatial relationship, timing, power, rhythm, and speed. From here the attacker proceeds to striking in sets of two strikes, which the defender must block and counter—and so on through twelve strikes. At later stages of this practice, various strikes will be used (as opposed to mere direct striking), such as with the butt-end of the stick and the empty-hand.

From this basic drilling comes the so-called "groupings." Again, the philosophy of Balintawak is that of assuming an opponent will be able to effectively block and counter some of your strikes. The groupings thus offer practitioners the ability to explore their counter and re-counter options. It is through these training drills that the art's four categories of defense are realized.

The first defensive category finds the practitioner blocking the opponent's stick with his stick, checking the opponent's attacking limb or weapon with his non-dominant (or empty) hand, and then counter striking with his stick.

The second defensive category finds the practitioner blocking the opponent's stick with his stick and then immediately counter striking with the same stick in the next beat. This category omits the non-dominant hand checking, thus making the sequence faster than the previous.

The third defensive category finds the practitioner utilizing a simultaneous attack and defensive maneuver. In other words, both the checking hand and striking weapon come into play in the same instance, thus being efficient and difficult to counter.

The fourth defensive category finds the practitioner at once evading an attack while directly striking the attacker's body or attacking limb. This is the most efficient defensive maneuver as it is the most difficult to defend against.

The basic strikes, blocks, and counters, and the four defensive categories are all trained through the nucleus "grouping" drills. When performed "at random" these drills become like fighting, as every movement is spontaneous and nothing is predetermined.

Power in striking, proper body mechanics, and endurance are developed by striking a rubber car tire or heavy bag with the stick for extended periods of time.

Fighting Strategies

Balintawak Arnis is an art primarily based in fighting strategies and movement concepts. As such, there are a number of articulated fighting strategies employed by practitioners to defeat their opponents.

The first order of business is how to face an opponent in various ranges. When in long range, practitioners stand with their body turned sideways. This position severely limits the opponent's target selection, thus forcing him to strike at less-than-ideal targets. When in close range, the body is turned almost square to the opponent, thus affording the practitioner the ability to concurrently use both hands for attack and defense.

It is the strategy of controlling the distance between opponents and the range of combat that often leads the Balintawak practitioner to victory. Many styles are only versed in a single range of combat, so in Balintawak the range in which the opponent is strongest is avoided.

The next strategy comes into play once the fighting gap has been bridged and the combatants are in a range wherein either or both may be hit. At this stage the system's five principles of attack come into play.

The first principle is that of taking the initiative and striking first. This strategy allows the practitioner to "get the jump" on his opponent, while eliminating the possibility that he may not be able to effectively counter the opponent's first strike. In other words, the best defense is a dynamic offense.

The second principle follows the first and finds the practitioner striking his opponent at various angles and levels. In an effort to not lose the element of surprise while also keeping the opponent confused and mentally "off-balance," the Balintawak practitioner will follow his initial strike with another strike in the opposite area. In other words, attack high to draw a response and then low to hit the newly-created opening.

The third principle of attack is similar to the second, except it presupposes that your initial strike has been blocked by the opponent. Whereas the second principle encourages opposite strikes, the third principle finds the practitioner striking at any angle that is uncovered once the opponent's block has contacted your stick. In other words, if blocked, keep changing striking angles at high speeds to keep the opponent from blocking all of the strikes.

The fourth principle is that of striking the target that is nearest to you. Thus, if the opponent is leaning forward, strike his head, and if his weapon hand is within reach, strike that directly.

The fifth attacking principle is to always strike in combination, and never assume a single blow will land, let alone end the confrontation. In other words, whether the opponent blocks your first strike or not, keep striking along various angles until he is out of commission.

Should the gap be closed and the Balintawak practitioner's strikes be blocked, another strategy is found within the fighting techniques themselves. This is a strategy of combining blocks, checks, parries, and strikes in various ways to place oneself in a safe position while at the same time opening the opponent's defense for a finishing combination. Such techniques include: blocking stick-to-stick and then grabbing the opponent's weapon with the empty hand to control it while countering with the weapon—a method known as *sabling*; blocking stick-to-stick and then parrying the opponent's weapon with the empty hand to open an area in which to counter attack unobstructed—a method known as *tukas;* after the opponent block your strike and grabs your stick, you in turn push the opponent's stick down to strike his own wrist—a method known as *suyop;* and blocking stick-to-stick and then parrying his weapon in its intended direction, clearing your weapon, and counter striking along the same angle—a method known as *yakap.*

Free-Sparring

While there is no free-sparring "train-ing" *per se* in Balintawak Arnis, most of the training is done in sponta-neous, two-person drills. Thus, from the onset the novice develops the skills to attack, defend, respond, and react in spontaneous, "at random" ways, with little structure to the

exchanges. It can be said, then, that the training itself is free-sparring, while true application is carried out in life-and-death encounters.

In addition to the realistic drills and free-flow exchanges between opponents, many practitioners of Balintawak Arnis do compete in full-contact tournaments against practitioners from other schools. This, however, is considered sport and not real, as the targets are limited and the participants padded.

Grandmaster Abner G. Pasa

4

BALITOK ESKRIMA

Balitok Eskrima was founded and developed in Cebu, Philippines by Abner Pasa. It is Pasa's personal fighting style, and is taught only on a one-to-one basis. When training the masses, other methods of Eskrima are taught under the banner "Warrior's Eskrima." As a style, Balitok makes wide use of feinting techniques, resulting in its practitioners often being called *lansidors* (feintors) by other *eskrimadors*. The term *balitok* was adopted as the deceptiveness of its techniques resembles the attacking methods of a Filipino snake, or *balitok*.

Training Progressions

In terms of distance, the first category of training in Balitok Eskrima is projectile weapons. Although the art does not use the bow-and-arrow or throwing spears, practitioners do practice knife throwing. This is followed by flexible weapons training, in which the whip and the chain are practiced. Next comes rigid weapons, which includes the use of four- and six-foot staffs, *kampilan* sword, single stick, double sticks, *espada y daga,* and knife.

While the above categories are incorporated into Balitok Eskrima's curriculum, the specialization of the art is the single stick and knife. And in addition to weapons training, the system also incorporates Pangamut, the empty hand art of kicking, close-quarter striking, joint locking, and choking.

Since in their early stages of training students generally want to train with weapons they can relate to in a realistic self-defense situation, the single stick is taught first, followed by empty hand defenses against the knife. It is only after these weapons are learned that the more classical weapon combinations, such as

double sticks and stick/sword and dagger are taught, as most beginners struggle to appreciate their relevance in modern times.

Beginners are first made aware of how they may be attacked through the use of Balitok's twelve angles of attack. The numbering system is then used as a framework in which to practice defensive movements through evasion and body angling. Once a student can defend himself competently, counter techniques such as striking, disarming, locking, and throwing are taught.

Through dedicated practice, students are able to increase

their level of coordination and develop an appreciation of body mechanics and weapon awareness. At this point, pre-arranged two-man drills are introduced and are excellent for developing reflexes, timing, and coordination.

It is only after practitioners can perform the drills with proficiency that they are introduced to free-sparring, which familiarizes them with the chaos and unpredictability of a real fight. It is here that students learn to adapt and improvise—or simply "go with the flow." Skills such as understanding distance and employing feints to create openings are developed in the free-sparring matches.

Training Methods

Balitok Eskrima utilizes a drill known as *palakaw* (lit., "to walk freely"), as a basic training method. And while the drill may resemble those found in other styles, it is the progression and intricacies as it is performed in this art that set it apart. As performed in Balitok Eskrima, this drill allows one to hone his sensitivity, reflexes, timing, and line familiarization to a high degree. *Palakaw* is generally practiced in close-to-medium ranges with the stick, knife, double sticks, and stick and dagger. In essence, the drill develops trapping skills and makes practitioners aware of the other tools that can be utilized in a fight, such as punching with the "live" or less-dominant hand, low line kicking, and sweeping.

Single and double stick solo forms, generically called *amara*, are also an integral part of training. These are introduced early on in training as they teach students the basics of manipulating their weapons. The *amara* are taught in ten sets and familiarize students with the various strikes in the system and are great for developing hand speed. The late Filemon

Cañete's San Miguel solo form is also incorporated into the system and is practiced to develop *espada y daga* skills, coordination, and footwork. Solo forms are important for skills development as they allow one to practice without dependence on a training partner.

There are also a number of single stick training drills found in Balitok Eskrima. At long range, drills known as *singko-singko* (five/five) are practiced. These drills find one person executing five attacks while the partner employs five counters, one for each attack. The drills utilize the thrust for attacking and are excellent for developing distance appreciation and footwork.

At medium range, a set of drills incorporated from Balintawak Arnis known as *pakgang/agak* (to "give and take") are practiced. These drills develop recovery skills after striking, which in turn highlight the importance of good blocking skills.

Where the knife is concerned, a drill known as *tapi-tapi* (tapping or checking) is utilized to help practitioners develop a defensive shield around the body, and is practiced knife against empty hands and knife against knife. It is held that when facing a blade, one's skills must be highly developed, as even a small cut from a knife can be potentially deadly. Since the knife is a close range weapon, the defensive motions become much tighter and smaller than with the stick. This understanding forces students when practicing this drill to be quick and acutely sensitive.

It must be noted that the drills in Balitok Eskrima are viewed as merely stepping stones to the ultimate test of the art: free-sparring. As Abner Pasa is fond of saying: "You use a drill to instill a skill. Learn the skill and forget the drill. You fight with your skill and not your drill."

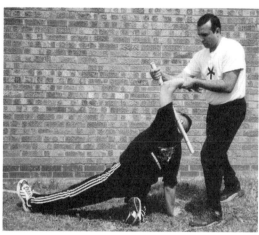
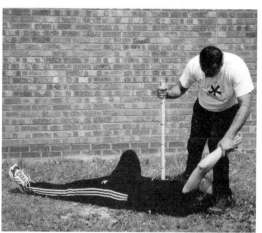

Fighting Strategies

There are a number of principles found in Balitok Eskrima that effect the application of technique. The first is to develop an awareness of, and adapt to, the nature of the environment in which the combative encounter is taking place. For example, in areas in the Philippines where rice fields dominate, a linear style of movement is prevalent, as rice fields are characterized by narrow and slippery pathways. The layout of those pathways are linear and at points where pathways intersect, the layout is angular. The same can be observed of the alleyways found in most major cities.

In other areas where the terrain is characterized by narrow paths with heavy undergrowth on one or both sides, one can rely heavily on thrusts, rather than the more natural slashing motions. For example, in such an environment, if an opponent feigns a strike, and you were to respond with a fully committed slash as a defense, then your weapon would end up entangled in the undergrowth, thus giving the opponent time to counter. A more effective response would be to thrust.

Essentially, Balitok Eskrima is characterized by stable stances and a reliance on strength. Blocking is predominant, while parries are generally used against thrusting attacks. Evading blows are usually done with body angling and ducking, rather than with overt body movement, or the transference of the body from one location to another. Slashing blows in this system do not describe a full arc and are seldom delivered with full force, as practitioners believe that the risk of losing one's balance is magnified if one executes slashes in this manner. The thrust is generally not executed for the same reason.

Another important principle found in Balitok Eskrima is that one must develop an appreciation for the characteristics of the weapon being used. For example, a long blade such as a *pinute* and a regular rattan *baston* (stick) have different charac-

teristics, thus effecting their use—one is edged and the other is not. Yet, many *eskrimadors* fail to understand or appreciate this. For example, while styles favoring curved strikes are effective in close-quarter fighting with sticks, the same curved strikes would be impossible to execute with bladed weapons. Moreover, if one tries snapping techniques known as *witik* using a bladed weapon, they will not hit their opponent with the sharp edge but with the flat side of the blade.

Once practitioners of Balitok Eskrima have a thorough understanding of these principles they are able to adapt their style to any given environment or situation, while at the same time maximizing the effectiveness of the weapons they employ.

Free-Sparring

Senior students of Balitok Eskrima spend the majority of their time engaging in free-sparring practice. At long range, padded sticks are used. The only target sought after in this range is the weapon-holding hand or the lead leg. And since the sticks themselves are padded, no protective gloves are worn. Sparring sessions consist of one minute rounds, with emphasis on evasion through footwork and body swaying.

At medium range, a light headguard is worn. While the padded sticks are still used in this range, targets are increased to encompass the entire body. The emphasis at medium range is to develop good blocking skills with the stick, then to control your opponent's weapon with your "live" hand and counter attack.

At close range, the *punyo,* or butt-end of the stick, is extensively used for striking. Takedown techniques are also employed in this range.

When using unpadded rattan sticks and wearing no body armor, practitioners of Balitok Eskrima engage in controlled free-sparring. It is in this arena that emphasis is placed on mastery of skills, wherein one must be able to control their strikes even when delivering them at high speeds. At this level it is not necessary to hit your opponent, as a good *eskrimador* will recognize if his defense has been penetrated. Indeed, many of the older masters in the Philippines spar this way with their students on a regular basis.

Master Alfredo Bandalan

5

BANDALAN DOCE PARES ESKRIMA

The Bandalan system of Doce Pares Eskrima was developed by Alfredo Bandalan as an outgrowth of his studies in the multi-style Doce Pares system of Dionisio "Dioney" Cañete, the modern Eskrido system of Ciriaco "Cacoy" Cañete, and his additional studies in Cabales Serrada Escrima and Hawaiian-Chinese Kenpo. As a system, Bandalan Doce Pares trains the use of the single stick *(solo olisi)*, double sticks *(doble olisi)*, empty hands *(mano y mano)*, sword and dagger *(espada y daga)*, knife *(baraw)*, and is augmented with the systems of Eskrido (weapon grappling), Dumog (unarmed grappling), and Pangamot (striking and kicking).

Training Progressions

Students progress through the curriculum along the lines of their titles: basic, intermediate, high intermediate, and advanced. At the basic level, students are taught the history

49

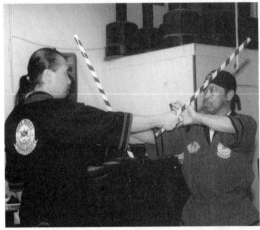

of the Doce Pares Association of Cebu, class rules, various Filipino customs, and the meaning of the art's salutation. The key custom and salutation finds the younger person approaching and taking the elder's hand and touching the back of the hand to his forehead as he bends to one knee. This denotes a request for the elder's blessing, and shows to others that the younger holds a high respect for the elder.

Stick manipulations are taught with the overlap and reverse gripping methods. In addition to being adaptable, the overlap grip is the most widely used in Eskrima today as it offers maximum control in all striking angles and directions and is secure against slippage even in extreme situations. The reverse grip is the opposite of the overlap grip, and usually comes into play as a result of an emergency situation or from the application of a disarming technique. This grip finds the weapon tip protruding down from the pinky, as opposed to up from the thumb.

The twelve basic strikes are then learned and practiced from the modified *corto* and the *abesedario*. The modified *corto* was developed by Cacoy Cañete, and is considered a modern style of Eskrima as it concentrates on close range fighting. This style brings into play the techniques of *corto kurbada,* or the curving strikes that Cacoy used in his so-called "death matches." These strikes include the top of the head, right and left temples, right and left ribs, right and left elbows, right and left knees, right and left sides of the chest, and the abdomen.

The basic counters are logically placed to wherever the angle of attack is coming from. The modified *corto*, which is the simplest style, is based on returning the counter back to the same target your opponent was striking towards. The practitioner then continues by striking to the opposite side of the target, until his opponent is out of commission or blocks the subsequent counter. If the opponent succeeds in blocking the counter, the Bandalan practitioner again changes his striking angle to strike an unprotected part of the opponent's body.

The *abesedario* is the baseline or foundation of the Bandalan system, just as it is part of the original multi-system of Doce Pares. On a fundamental level, *abesedario* consists of the following twelve strikes, or angles of attack: right then left temples, right then left shoulders, right then left sides of the abdomen, right then left knees, right then left sides of the chest, right then left attacks to the top of the head.

The *abesedario* is then further divided into twelve variations, as practiced with both single and double sticks. These are: linear, *orihinal*, reverse grip, reverse footwork, *corto orihinal* (old style of the Saavedra clan), *larga mano* (Eulogio Cañete's long range method), *corto kurbada* (Cacoy's close range method), *espada y daga* (Filemon Cañete's method), *baraw* (Vicente Carin's knife fighting method), Eskrido, Pangamot, and Dumog.

The basic stick manipulations, strikes, blocks, and counters are first performed from the following nine stances: the attention or close stance, natural stance, forward stance, deep forward stance, diagonal stance, back stance, cat stance, hook stance, and straddle stance. There are a number of fighting stances, as each is used depending on the dictates of the situation and one's reaction to an opponent's movement.

The relevance of stances to footwork is also taught at the beginning level, and how they each relate to specific fighting situations. Of course, students begin their training of strikes, blocks, and counters while in solid stances. On progressing, they are taught the system's footwork and how it relates to each movement and situation. Footwork maneuvers include sliding steps, hook steps, and V-shape steps, all done forward, backward, side-to-side, and in circles.

Upon completing the basic level, students progress to the intermediate level, wherein they are taught defensive and offensive techniques combined with various methods of disarming. At this level they are also introduced to the *amara* striking combinations, proper methods of rolling and break-falling with and without a weapon, and the first three of the system's twelve pre-arranged solo forms. And if a student is competent enough, he may opt to participate in controlled sparring sessions.

Upon perfecting the material of the previous levels, a student may be promoted to the rank of high intermediate, wherein bladed weapons are introduced into the curriculum. At this level, students learn the fundamental methods of empty hand knife defenses, and the knife against knife fighting techniques of Vicente Carin—who is somewhat of a living legend in Cebu for surviving multiple knife fights. In addition to the knife, techniques and methods of various swords, such as the *kris, bolo,* and *kampilan* are introduced. Disarming techniques and their reversals for both knife and sword are also taught.

Students progress to the advanced level only when their skill in all the aforementioned areas is close to mastery. In the advanced level is found offensive and defensive empty hand combinations with low-line kicking techniques, the complete set of twelve forms, including the five-and-a-half minute San Miguel form of Filemon Cañete. The skills and knowledge of advanced empty hand joint locks and throws, in addition to the stick locking and throwing methods of Eskrido are also taught at this level.

While there is no pre-set time limit a student must spend on a given level before advancing to the next, they are encouraged to take as much time as necessary to display acceptable proficiency at every level. On the average, though, students tend to spend one year on each level before moving on.

Training Methods

Bandalan Doce Pares Eskrima utilizes a number of training drills to enhance in its practitioners the necessary attributes of combat. These drills find themselves in the forms of solo exercises and partner drills, both pre-arranged and improvised.

The primary methods for developing striking combinations are *sinawali* and *amara*. *Sinawali* are pre-set, two-person combinations of three or more strikes per side, performed with double sticks. Not only does *sinawali* train left/right hand combinations, but also hand/eye coordination, flow, timing, speed, body angling, control of distance to move in and out of combat ranges, and the ability to evade an opponent's strikes.

Amara, on the other hand, are solo striking combinations developed in two phases. Students first learn the numerous twirling combinations in the air. After perfecting the movements, they progress to the tire stacks and heavy bag, where they apply the *amara* strikes against hard objects. The tires stacks quickly build striking power while also developing control as the rubber tires tend to bounce the stick back toward the practitioner when striking is done incorrectly. The heavy bag, which is swung back and forth, develops proper footwork in combination with striking, in addition to awareness of range and spacing when applying striking

combinations while gaining more power and speed when attacking. These develop in practitioners stamina, hand/foot coordination, the linking of footwork with various types and methods of strikes and their related defenses, and the power of visualization.

Amara are related to *karenza,* the art's pre-arranged fighting forms, of which there are twelve. Students are given the freedom to use whatever weapon they are proficient in and incorporate it into the form of their choice—thus illustrating the universal application of movements found in the forms, and indeed in the system. *Karenza* are an integral part of a student's development and a great source of future growth for the Bandalan system.

While each of the dozen forms has its specific focus, when taken as a whole they are geared toward developing reflexes and the skills necessary to defeat multiple attacks and opponents. They are usually performed against two or more imaginary opponents—again developing visualization skills—and are ideal methods of developing footwork, body mechanics and angulation, hand techniques, and complex weapon twirling and circular strikes.

Another key two-person training method is the *tapi-tapi* or hand-checking drills. *Tapi-tapi* is a series of drills that develop the so-called "live hand," the secondary or non-dominant hand. This set of drills is integral to the system as the skills of the "live hand" are employed in nearly every technique in the art. The drills begin with partners moving through pre-arranged sequences of techniques, with speed and intensity increasing with skill level. After a high degree of skill is attained, practitioners then engage in free-flow or improvised *tapi-tapi,* wherein none of the strikes or sequences are pre-arranged, thus developing skills in reacting and countering to an "alive" opponent.

Fighting Strategies

The articulated fighting strategies of the Bandalan system are few but nonetheless effective. On a fundamental level, practitioners intuit and come to discover methods of outmaneuvering their opponent through the practice of the solo forms and partner drills.

One of the primary fighting strategies is to employ the modified *corto (corto kurbada)* in combination with the *abesedario* variations in medium and long fighting ranges. This strategy affords the practitioner the ability to bait his opponent at different ranges to draw him into a position of weakness, which is then fully exploited.

Another strategy is found in the *Sabayan* philosophy, which states that one should never retreat or retract their strikes when fighting. Simply explained, the stick or weapon does not retract when encountering a block or hindrance. It simply changes angles by the manipulation of the practitioner's wrist, who employs the *corto kurbada* to strike the new opening made available by the opponent's attempt to block the initial strike.

A third strategy is to take the opponent by surprise by employing Western boxing techniques in the midst of weapons combat. As this is an unexpected tactic, the opponent will generally be ill prepared to deal with such techniques and thus unable to defend against them.

Free-Sparring

Bandalan Doce Pares Eskrima holds free sparring as the ultimate test of a practitioner's knowledge and skill. In essence, sparring finds one practitioner putting into play all of his acquired and developed skills and knowledge to outmaneuver his opponent.

As a classical fighting art and modern fighting sport, the Bandalan system embraces sparring on two levels: controlled and full-contact. In controlled sparring, no body armor is worn. Thus, attacks and counters are executed to their intended targets but are stopped short of contact. This method of sparring is useful in initiating students into the realm of fighting without fear of serious injury. Moreover, as no protection is worn, this method develops precision in technique and timing.

Full-contact sparring, on the other hand, is practiced all-out. As such, full protective body armor is worn to help prevent or lessen possible injuries. This method of sparring initiates practitioners to the real-world clash of an actual weapons fight, while at the same time developing their striking power, stamina, and warrior mind-set.

There are three stages to learning how to spar within the two aforementioned levels. First, practitioners are required to engage in pre-arranged sparring. Second, practitioners are introduced to *corto kurbada* or close quarter sparring with light

contact. And third, practitioners engage in full-contact sparring from any range and using any combination of techniques they like.

Grandmaster Carlos Navarro

6

BLACK EAGLE
ARNIS-ESKRIMA

The Black Eagle Arnis-Eskrima system was founded by Carlos Navarro in Cebu City, Philippines, in the 1960s. It is a system based on the essence of two classical styles—Eskrima de Llave and Eskrima de Avaniko—and a third modern style developed by Navarro known simply as New Generation. The techniques, training, and applications of Black Eagle are trained and employed through solo and paired drills in long, medium, and short ranges.

Training Progressions

There are several categories of training in Black Eagle Arnis-Eskrima, including single stick, double sticks, staff, single dagger, double daggers, stick and dagger, and empty hands. The art also makes use of swords and a flail called *de cadena,* but these are taught only to the most advanced practitioners. Many of the drills for each weapon category are also sub-grouped by one of the three styles which make up the foundation of this system: Eskrima de Llave (the key), Eskrima de Avanico (the fan), and New Generation. It should be noted that these styles are not taught as isolated entities, but as conceptual components embodying elements of what were once separate systems.

Pangamot, Black Eagle's empty hand art, includes both wrist and arm locking techniques, with thumb and finger locks as specialties. It also employs a series of fundamental throwing exercises called "four direction throws" or "touches." Ground fighting and various striking techniques including hammer fist strikes, low kicks, and knee strikes are also taught in Pangamot.

Formal rank is used and is divided into four levels: beginner, junior instructor, senior instructor, and master. Progression through the ranks is generally a matter of talent, rather than time or knowledge. Advanced students can learn most aspects of the curriculum at any time they wish, as there is a relaxed attitude toward teaching this art, with no set time limit to class length or rank advancement.

As a general guideline, however, beginners are first introduced to the system's twelve strikes, its single stick form, double stick twirling motions known as *amara,* and the New Generation long range defense drill. In addition to the weapon techniques, basic Pangamot defenses and locks from lapel grabs, holds, and punches are also taught from the onset of training. After the long range New Generation drill is perfected, students progress to the short range New Generation drills, as New Generation transits but does not fight at middle range. This is followed by de Llave techniques at medium range. The staff is also a de Llave style weapon, and is introduced to students as part of their basic training.

After an understanding of hand smashing defenses of New Generation and the augmented blocks of de Llave, students are introduced to stick grappling, knife defenses, weapon disarming, and sparring exercises. Two-man forms are practiced by senior instructors.

Training Methods

There are several interesting training methods used in Black Eagle Arnis-Eskrima, ranging from solo and partner practice to pre-arranged and free-flow movements. A posture known as the "eagle eye" involves holding the weapon at eye level and pointing it toward an imaginary opponent. From this position, practitioners look at the end of their stick (as if looking down the barrel of a gun) and imagine the opponent beyond. This posture develops an awareness of weapon length, indicates the maximum range for hitting, and develops emotional intensity for fighting.

Although Black Eagle utilizes double sticks, it actively rejects the rhythmic symmetrically partnered sinawali drills found in many other Filipino arts. Instead, its practitioners prefer to train what they call "double stick clatter." This drill, the movements of which derive primarily from the stick and dagger, teaches how to use the

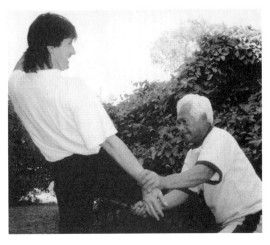

dagger to control an opponent's weapon. Students move back and forth in a set pattern of block and counter techniques wherein the position, use, and placement of the dagger (or second stick) is paramount. The sound of the sticks indicates

the broken rhythm nature of the exercise. The drill also teaches footwork and body shaping and provides the technical foundation for short range single stick and empty hand sparring.

The "battle attack" drill involves a simple striking pattern of multiple forehand and/or backhand diagonal and horizontal slashes. To perform this drill, students begin in a ready posture and on the instructor's command charge forward, slashing rapidly in this pattern. This drill is repeated over and over. Students are not to look at their stick while swinging but past it at an imaginary opponent.

Another set of drills develops defensive skills against the primary striking patterns used by contemporary schools of arnis, such as Lapunti Arnis de Abaniko, Balintawak Arnis, and Doce Pares Eskrima. As an example, the attacker may execute continuous vertical, circular strikes (the *redonda* of Lapunti) while the defender counters with the New Generation striking patterns. The drill develops in students a sense of timing for when to hit an opponent's hand when employing such a technique.

Black Eagle Arnis-Eskrima uses pre-arranged solo forms for training the empty hands, single stick, double short sticks, double sticks, and staff. All solo forms begin with the "eagle

eye" and follow a pre-set combination of strikes. As practitioners advance, they are encouraged to mix up or otherwise improvise the striking patterns ("battle attack"), changing them at will to develop their ability to not get stuck on the pattern but move freely as the situation dictates. After a convenient number of steps, students stop and do what is known as "four corner striking" (multiple opponent techniques), return to their starting position while striking along various angles, followed again by "four corner striking," and then turning and advancing. The practitioner stops in a position in the middle between the two places they did the four corner movements and employs twirling strikes, moving around forward and backward, imagining that they are keeping opponents at bay. The form finishes with a thrust. These forms are important exercises as they combine all the basic movements with footwork and tactics for single and multiple opponent confrontations—tactics later drilled in sparring.

Black Eagle Arnis-Eskrima also employs two-person forms known as "exhibition fighting." These forms were actually introduced into the system so that it would have captivating movements to demonstrate in public. Be that as it may, the two-person forms do contain the basis of advanced principles disguised beneath the flashy movements. These are explained to advanced practitioners but are virtually invisible to most viewers. The two-person forms are taught in the following combinations: empty hands against empty hands; empty hands against single dagger; empty hands against double daggers; single stick against single stick; double sticks against double sticks; double sticks against staff; and staff against staff.

After learning the preliminary striking motions and combining these with footwork in the solo forms, students are introduced to the basic empty hand skills of twisting, locking, throwing, and sweeping. The characteristics of these skills is such that they can be performed as readily with as without a weapon. The techniques are first applied against punches and grabs and then against dagger or stick attacks. This is performed much the same as another core flow drill called "back and forth," wherein one partner disarms an attack and then counterattacks with the weapon, the other partner then responds in kind, and so on.

The tire dummy is also heavily utilized to develop both speed and power for effective sparring combinations. This is a multi-level structure of tires that is struck with various weapons at various angles.

Fighting Strategies

Black Eagle's set techniques, like the name of one of its sub-styles—de Llave—do provide a "key" for the dedicated student to unlock more advanced techniques. The underlying concepts, particularly those inherent in the three sub-styles, aim to make practitioners adaptable to any situation, as the deeper the understanding of the underlying principles and concepts, the more techniques can be improvised. In fact, practitioners believe that to try and rigidly define each and every possible technique and permutation is to kill the spontaneity of the flow and to miss the point.

The three styles and their individual characteristics provide a way of teaching the different combat concepts. Each style has its own personality and provides principles for handling different weights and lengths of weapons, ranges and types of opponents. What you can do with light rattan may not be the same when wielding a length of two-by-four. Thus, New Generation and de Avanico are best performed with a light stick, whereas de Llave is more adaptable to long, heavy, or flexible weapons. The three styles, therefore, teach the concept of adaptability to any circumstance and with any weapon.

Feeling that the classical Arnis and Eskrima styles rely too heavily on block-and-then-counter techniques—a two beat process—Navarro developed the New Generation style, which is characterized by aggressive stop hitting. In other words: strike first, ask questions later. A stop hit with rapid multiple follow-ups, particularly to the weapon-holding hand, can stop a fight at the onset. As such, this style employs only direct striking techniques, such as a swift jab-like backhand strike, and hammering blows designed to cut into attacks to destroy an attacker's capacity for wielding his weapon. Footwork and body shaping must be used to accommodate such techniques and is characterized by charging forward on various angles.

The de Llave style is characterized by its application of blocks, strikes, and locks while maintaining or changing various grips on the stick. Since it is a block-and-counter or block-and-lock style, it is best employed with relatively heavy or long weapons, including chains. As a result of the weapon's weight, it is swung from the shoulder rather than the elbow or wrist. At long range, de Llave makes use of deceptive, irregular winding patterns, known as the "winding style." Although primarily a fighting style for longer weapons, the key of de

Llave is its in-fighting techniques, for which there is a sophisticated system of locks, chokes, and takedowns with the stick.

This grip change facilitates the raking motions used for disarming, the capturing and locking of limbs, and applying stick chokes. As such, practitioners are able to strike rapidly with either end of their weapon when in short range and then lock the opponent. The stick locks are designed to unbalance the opponent enough to open him up for a decisive blow or expose his groin or throat to a knee or elbow strike. Hand exchanges are also common in de Llave locking techniques.

The de Avanico style is characterized by fast, fan-like movements, wherein the stick can strike on many angles in a matter of seconds, quickly moving around an opponent's guard. At the same time, the left hand (either empty or holding a dagger) can be used to strike or immobilize the opponent's weapon. De Avinico is a nimble style wherein the dagger (or any weapon) held in the left hand is used to facilitate blocking and trapping of an opponent's weapon while simultaneously striking with the stick. On other occasions the stick is used to either press down an opponent's arm to expose his neck to a dagger thrust or to lift up the opponent's arm to expose his armpit. The simultaneous use of stick and dagger allows simultaneous blocks and strikes.

Free-Sparring

Free-sparring is practiced in both long and short ranges, with single and double sticks, against both single and multiple opponents. Many types of protective equipment have been experimented with over the years, some very light. This still continues to evolve.

Bruising contact sparring to a full-body target is an essential ingredient of the training program. Sparring is done in various

ways. In short range, practitioners start facing each other with their hands touching each other's weapons. While short range sparring, practitioners always consider that a blade may be in play and so do not attempt to crash body to body, but stay at arm's length. Practitioners learn how to hit at short range without exposing their arm to a counter strike or disarm—a skill called "hiding the hand."

At long range, sparring is less structured and considered free-for-all. Fighters first attempt to stay at long range, but, depending on the opponent's reactions and counters, they move in and out of long, medium, and short ranges, blending techniques from the three basic styles as required.

Multiple opponent sparring finds one person in the middle of a circle comprising three-to-four students. Using multiple opponent techniques from the solo form, the defender has to keep the others at bay, avoid getting hit, and striking them as they come in.

Grandmaster Angel Cabales

7

Cabales Serrada Escrima

The Cabales Serrada Escrima system was developed in the mid-1960s by the late Angel Cabales. While a teenager living in Cebu, Cabales studied boxing and later de Cuerdas Escrima under Felicisimo Dizon. Upon relocating to the United States, Cabales systematized the de Cuerdas style and added an empty hand aspect he had not previously learned from Dizon, thus creating the Cabales Serrada system.

Training Progressions

Cabales Serrada Escrima is a system that is compact both in terms of movement and curriculum. There are three levels of rank within the art—basic, advanced, master—in which different levels of information are learned, and built from the foundation of the previous level. While originally a stick and dagger art, single stick training has come to the forefront. With a foundation in single stick techniques, students then learn the empty hands, single knife, and then stick and dagger.

Beginners are first taught how to measure their stick, which equals the length of an extended arm from the armpit to the wrist. They are then taught how to assume the basic fighting stance, how to maneuver along an isosceles triangle pattern, and how to execute the system's twelve angles of attack.

Once these basics are learned, three basic single stick defenses against the first five angles of attack are taught. After angle five is learned, practitioners move on to the system's core training drills, known as "lock and block" and "flow sparring." After a level of sufficient skill is achieved with the basic techniques in these drills, three basic single stick defenses against the remaining seven angles of attack are then learned.

During the course of training, and left to the desecration of the instructor, practitioners are taught three basic empty hand parries, a set of sixteen basic joint locking techniques, and how to disarm an opponent while performing the above-mentioned counters. It is at this point that a student will be graduated to the rank of basic instructor, and receive the "basic degree" certificate.

To be awarded the "advanced degree," a practitioner must be able to demonstrate between six and fourteen single stick counters against each of the twelve angles of attack, be able to perform disarms during the course of each counter, be able to incorporate the new techniques into the "lock and block" drill and use and defend against them in "flow sparring." In addition to the new defensive techniques, practitioners at this level are also taught methods of feinting or drawing openings in an opponent's defenses—a skill known as "picking"—as well countering an opponent's counters of his techniques—a skill known as "reversing."

To be graduated with the "masters degree," practitioners of Cabales Serrada Escrima must demonstrate perfect execution of all of the preceding blocks and counters in the system, as well as articulate their finer points and theories. As regarding

new material, techniques in the knife, stick and dagger, methods of maneuvering from the inside to the outside and from the outside to the inside of an opponent's attacks, and methods for countering a long stick with the system's short stick are introduced. It is at this point that a student's training is said to be complete.

Training Methods

A primary method of training the blocking techniques finds practitioners pairing off, with one attacking and the other blocking and countering. After the basic counters have been perfected, practitioners move on to the art's three principal drills, which leads them to be able to apply block and counter techniques in an appropriate and reflexive manner.

The first drill is known as "lock and block," and refers to a "locked" or "set" fighting guard, which assumes lateral movement of the practitioner's arms and weapons to overcome inertia, thus allowing one to respond more quickly to a given attack. As with basic defense training, "lock and block" begins with two partners facing one another—one is the defender; the other is the attacker. The defender is armed with a single stick, and must effectively defend himself against an opponent aggressively wielding both a stick and dagger. In the initial levels of this drill, the defender's goal is to block the attacker's stick attack, complete an entire counter sequence, and return to his "locked" position prior to the initiation of the attacker's follow-up dagger thrust. At this level, the attacker strikes in sequence (i.e., angle one, dagger thrust,

angle two, dagger thrust, angle three, etc.). During the latter stages of the drill, the attacker strikes and thrusts at will, thus forcing the defender to depend on honed reflexive actions to support his transition from one counter sequence to the next without hesitation or disruption. At advanced stages, "lock and block" is performed with no attacking sequence, and with both attacker and defender armed with stick and dagger.

Another dill taught concurrently with "lock and block" is known as "flow sparring," which develops fundamental skills in single stick direct blocking and countering. This drill finds its participants facing off and engaging in an even exchange of strikes and blocks. That is, when one partner strikes, the second partner blocks, and when the second partner counter strikes, the first partner blocks. "Flow sparring" is primarily employed as a tool to teach practitioners how to block effectively and counter efficiently in a somewhat reflexive manner.

An advanced training drill is built around the techniques of "picking." While "picking" is a primary fighting strategy, when trained with a partner it becomes a drill to further develop reflexes and the ability to defend against such strikes. Practitioners are first taught how to properly execute the "picking" (or feinting) combinations and then how to time

 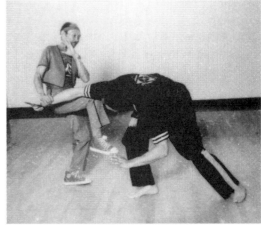

those of an opponent. This develops in the exponent the ability to decipher when an opponent has sufficiently committed to a strike, thus affording one the opportunity to "pick" him— or strike his open areas. In an effort to develop the skills and reflexes necessary to defend such strikes, one partner will execute single strikes against the other partner, who will counter. At an undetermined time the attacker will feint the first strike(s) and pick his opponent, who must then react accordingly and then follow up after the fakes have finished.

Fighting Strategies

Like the compact nature of the Cabales Serrada system itself, its number of articulated fighting strategies are also few, but nonetheless effective. Among the more prevalent are methods of controlling distance and spatial relationship through footwork, techniques of feinting for luring an opponent to commit to a false attack, and methods for countering an opponent's counter attack by going with the force of his strikes.

In terms of an overall basic strategy of maneuvering, practitioners step along standard isosceles triangles. To maneuver to the outside of an on-coming attack, practitioners step forward with their left leg along the left line of an inverted triangle. To face the on-coming attack, exponents replace their lead leg without changing distance, by stepping to the apex of the triangle with the rear leg and then back with the front leg. At times when an opponent's weapon is long or the Cabales Serrada exponent finds himself out of position, either a one-and-a-half stepping back combination or a series of short, stomping shuffle steps are used to adjust to the extra distance needed to move off the line of attack.

As described above, another key strategy used Cabales Serrada Escrima is known as "picking." This refers to methods of using fakes or feinting maneuvers to cause an opponent to open his guard in response to the false strikes, thus providing the attacker an opening to strike. Picks are executed as a series of strikes, and each of the system's twelve strikes has a specific picking combination that may be employed to fake the opponent.

If an opponent is able to effectively counter the Cabales Serrada exponent's attack, he employs techniques known as "reversing" to counter the opponent's counter. Such techniques include using the left hand or the stick to parry or pass the on-coming counter strike, followed immediately by striking along the newly-created open line of attack.

If the opponent is able to counter the counter, then the Serrada practitioner will employ the technique again, but in a different way, in an effort to end the exchange of strikes. This is known as "reverse reversing," or countering the counter. One method of "reverse reversing" that works well is known as "sticky stick," and refers to the method of blocking a strike with your stick and then immediately sliding your stick down the length of your opponent's stick in an attempt to strike his hand and disarm him.

Free-Sparring

Whereas "lock and block" teaches how to block multiple strikes effectively and then counter, and whereas "flow sparring" teaches how to block single strikes and counter with a single strike in return, and whereas "picking" teaches how to deliver feints and also block such strikes, they are not in themselves sparring. They are merely drills that individually develop specific skills and reflexes needed to survive an actual combative encounter.

Thus, Cabales Serrada Escrima practitioners combine the skills and techniques learned through their basics and drills in unarmored, light-contact, spontaneous sparring sessions. These find two opponents trying their best to strike the other without being struck themselves. And for those who are able, the techniques of disarming and joint locking may also be employed during the interaction. Sparring, then, is the ultimate test of one's true skills in this art.

Grandmaster Ely Pasco

8

D'KATIPUNAN ARNIS

D'Katipunan Arnis was developed by Ely Pasco of Bukidnon, Mindanao. Although he learned Arnis in Zamboanga del Sur as a teenager from his late brother, Silgerio Pasco, it was his encounter with the supernatural that inspired new techniques and spurred the development of his own fighting system.

Training Progressions

Training in D'Katipunan Arnis is primarily concerned with the use of the single stick, double sticks, and staff. The spear is also taught, but is considered a special weapon. In addition to these weapons, practitioners of this art also practice empty hand techniques of striking, disarming, and throwing lumped under the rubric term Combat Judo.

The first and perhaps most important thing students are taught upon entering this system is "the steppings," or methods of using footwork for attack, defense, and evasion. There are over a dozen basic defensive and offensive fighting techniques utilized in this art, each requiring a specific footwork.

Thus, footwork is emphasized from the onset of training.

Once footwork has been perfected the system's twelve angles of attack are taught, immediately followed by the offensive and defensive methods of the single stick, of which there are six: *doblete, eskriju, hirada Batangueña, hirada banda, banda y banda,* and *decuirdas.*

From here, the methods of the double sticks are learned, of which there are also six: *dublansa, bara y bara,* X1 and X2, *sapi-sapi or songkiti,* kangaroo, and praying mantis.

In total, there are twelve basic offensive and defensive methods taught in D'Katipunan Arnis. Within these twelve methods are found 156 fight-ing techniques, which become the art's fight-ing strategy. For prac-titioners who are able to master these twelve basic methods, an additional four may be taught, totaling sixteen stick fighting methods.

Once an understanding and level of skill is acquired with the double sticks, empty hand techniques are introduced into the curriculum. There are two divisions to the empty hand portion of D'Katipunan Arnis: locking and throwing techniques, loosely termed Combat Judo, and methods of disarming stick, knife, and gun. It should be noted that Combat Judo is a term to describe the locking techniques of several Arnis and Escrima systems, but has no connection to Japanese Judo proper.

Skills in the single stick, double sticks, and empty hands are considered essential as they are the most common types of encounters one may have to deal with in a self-defense situation. Thus, these elements are stressed over all others. Once the basics of these components are perfected, students engage in sparring practice known simply as "fencing."

For students wishing to master the art on the whole, the methods of stick fighting are then applied to the staff and spear, thus adding a more classical and artistic expression to D'Katipunan Arnis.

Training Methods

As students learn the techniques of D'Katipunan Arnis mainly by observation and repetition, only a few training methods are employed. In essence, an instructor will demonstrate and explain a new technique, after which students will pair up and take turns practicing the techniques against various strikes.

To develop timing and a sense of distance, the individual techniques are combined and executed in turn with a partner in give-and-take fashion. That is, one attacks and the other defends, and vice-versa.

Power and endurance are developed by repeatedly striking either a hanging or wall-mounted tire or a punching bag with the sticks and empty hands for specified periods of time.

Although training methods of few, practitioners of D'Katipunan Arnis feel that the most important elements to mastering their art are perfecting the basic offensive and defensive methods and applying those methods in un-padded, full-contact free-sparring sessions.

Fighting Strategies

There are twelve fighting strategies employed in D'Katipunan Arnis, as based on the twelve basic single stick and double stick offensive and defensive methods named above.

Regarding single stick methods, the strategies are: 1) *doblete,* wherein

a single block is followed by two counter strikes; 2) *eskriju,* which combines techniques of Eskrima and Combat Judo, wherein stick techniques are supplemented with joint locks and takedowns; 3) *hirada Batangueña,* wherein one evades or blocks a blow while simultaneously countering with his own weapon; 4) *hirada banda,* a direct attack made directly to the opponent's weapon-holding hand immediately followed by a strike to his head; 5) *banda y banda,* another hand and head striking combination, but while employing a side-stepping maneuver; and 6) *decuirdas,* an attack like a guitar string, wherein the attacking movement vibrates, as in multiple strikes in quick succession.

Regarding double stick methods, the strategies are: 1) *dublansa,* wherein one stick is used to deflect an attack while the other strikes the attacker; 2) *bara y bara,* which uses one short stick to attack with a thrust while the second short stick deflects the blow; 3) X defense, wherein the two sticks cross an attack in a scissors-like motion, one deflecting and the other slashing; 4) *sapi-sapi,* wherein the left stick blocks while the right stick attacks; 5) kangaroo, an attack wherein you jump toward an opponent like a kangaroo; and 6) praying mantis, an attack wherein the movements of a praying mantis are mimicked.

All techniques aside, practitioners of D'Katipunan Arnis hold that the key strategy in fighting is to never have to fight. When teaching, instructors often lecture students that in order to avoid confrontation one must live a simple life and never brag. Self-discipline, patience, and avoidance of conflict are stressed over physical skills.

Free-Sparring

Sparring practice is one of the two primary components to mastering the art of D'Katipunan Arnis; the other being mastery of the basics. When sparring, practitioners do their best to utilize the proper basics, execute clean techniques, employ the strategies of the twelve basic techniques, and to stand their ground even when struck by their opponent's weapon.

Grandmaster Jerson Tortal

9

DEKITI TIRSIA SIRADAS ARNIS

The Dekiti Tirsia Siradas Arnis system was founded in Negros Occidental, Philippines by Segundo Tortal in the early 1900s, and was handed down to his son, Conrado Tortal, who in turn passed it on to his son, Jerson "Nene" Tortal, the art's current headmaster. It is a close-quarters fighting art that is grounded in the style of *florete echikete,* and favors the use of bladed weapons.

Training Progressions

Dekiti Tirsia Siradas is a weapon-based system that makes use of single and double sticks, single and double knives, the *talibong* and *ginunting* swords, and the empty hands. Since weapons are considered an extension of the empty hands, empty hand fighting is viewed as the art's major component, while weapon fighting as the minor component.

Upon entering the system, students are taught how to strike along the art's twelve angles of attack in the air with the single stick. This is followed by striking along the same angles with the single stick again, but this time use the *punyo,* or butt end of the weapon.

Methods of footwork are introduced next, and include forward stepping, side stepping to the left and right, and stepping, body shifting, and pivoting from the inside to the outside and from the outside to the inside of an opponent's arm. It should be noted that there is no retreating footwork in Dekiti Tirsia Siradas, as repositioning through footwork and pivoting is employed to escape possible dangerous positions.

After the angles of attack and basic footwork are perfected, the two are combined, as it is believed that strikes and counters without footwork are useless. Thus, footwork is the key to effectively applying this art. In addition, proper body mechanics when stepping, pivoting, and striking are a must in order to deliver the strikes with sufficient power.

Since Dekiti Tirsia Siradas is a close-range fighting art, techniques are first taught from close range, followed by medium range, and then finally in long range. Thus, after strikes and footwork are integrated, students pair off and practice their counter and re-counter techniques with the single stick. After the basics and techniques have been perfected with the single stick, students repeat the training again with the sword and then yet again with the dagger. After these three fundamental weapon categories have been perfected, students can learn the double sticks, double knives, double sword, or empty hands, but at the instructor's discretion.

Since the majority of students entering Dekiti Tirsia Siradas come from other styles to learn specific components of this art, advancement in terms of techniques or rank is not pre-set, but dependent on the individual's skill and ability.

Training Methods

There are a number of training drills found in Dekiti Tirsia Siradas Arnis. In fact, there are nearly as many drills as there are techniques, as almost every technique with every weapon is trained in a drill. In essence, drills are performed by two partners in a three-count fashion: 1) attack, 2) counter attack, 3) counter of the counter, then repeat. This attack-counter-recounter-stop drilling method has been found to be essential to developing timing, distancing, and footwork with all types of weapons paired against one another.

Drilling generally follows the series of the twelve angles of attack and weapon progression. One student attacks along angle one with the single stick, the other student blocks and counters with a single stick, and the first student then counters the second's counter. This sequence then repeats on the opposite side, wherein partners switch roles (i.e., the defender becomes attacker and the attacker becomes defender). The angle two attack and defense is then drilled in the same manner, and so on until all twelve angles have been completed. The drilling then repeats along the sequence again, this time with the sword and then with the dagger, and so on.

Dekiti Tirsia Siradas is first and foremost a fighting art, and is therefore taught and learned primarily with a reacting partner. However, after the techniques have been learned and their finer points understood as a result of training them with a partner, they may be performed and linked into solo forms for practicing alone. However, while this may be good for solo practice, it is viewed as a less-than-ideal method of developing skill in the art for actual use against an alive, moving, and reacting opponent.

In addition to its curriculum for civilians, Dekiti Tirsia Siradas Arnis is also taught to Philippine military and law enforcement agencies. Understandably, whereas the civilian system maintains a lengthy curriculum, the military and law enforcement training is rather compact and short in terms of amount of time in training involved.

Emphasis in this setting is placed on efficient use of time and technique, and thus begins with knife fighting. Military and law enforcement personnel are first taught methods of fighting knife against knife, followed by knife against empty hands, empty hands against knife, and then stick against stick, stick against empty hands, and finally empty hands against stick.

This progression covers all the bases of the types of possible armed and unarmed situations one may encounter in these professions (excluding firearms). However, since most new recruits to these protection groups come in untrained, they are first drilled with wooden knives and then progress to dull, aluminum blades, and finally to fighting and defending against sharp, steel blades.

Fighting Strategies

The fighting strategies of Dekiti Tirsia Siradas are few, but nonetheless pertinent and interrelated. The most primary and basic of all strategies is to move off the line of an attack at all costs. This is achieved through an understanding and application of the system's footwork, pivoting, and body shifting.

A second strategy, and one that is an outgrowth out of the first, is to never go against the force of an attack when defending, but to go with its force. It is again the proper use of footwork, body weaving, and using the weapon to deflect rather than block that effects this strategy.

A third strategy, and another one built on the previous strategies, is that of directly striking an opponent's attacking limb from the onset of an attack. For example, if you are employing a stick, you would strike the opponent's attacking hand or wrist. If you are employing a bladed weapon, you would slice or cut the opponent's attacking arm or wrist. And if you are employing your empty hands, you would strike the opponent's attacking arm with a knife-hand chop. It is this initial attack to the on-coming limb that affords practitioners the ability to at once injure and off-balance an opponent at least long enough to execute a clean and effective counter attack to finish the altercation.

Free-Sparring

Free-sparring is the crux of Dekiti Tirsia Siradas Arnis. All of the training in the curriculum is performed with a partner and in free form drills, as opposed to pre-arranged two-person forms. It is believed that this method of training is the only way to develop realistic skills for sparring a "live" opponent or surviving a life-and-death encounter in the streets.

Beginners and female students are encouraged to wear body armor, headgear, or other types of protectors until such a time as they develop enough courage and skill to be able to spar with sticks while wearing no armor and using unpadded sticks. It is only through unarmored and realistic sparring by pairing various weapons against each other and against the empty hands that practitioners of this art feel one can truly develop the realistic skills and courage necessary to employ their art outside of the classroom or tournament setting and in the real world.

Grandmaster Jose Mena

10

Doblete Rapillon Arnis

Doblete Rapillon is a style of Arnis that Jose Mena inherited from his father, Patricio Mena, who in turn inherited it from his teacher, Carlos Haranella. The style became well-established in Manila, as Jose Mena was the first person to open a commercial club in the city's Tondo section in 1951. Aside from the use of the stick, sword, and dagger, Doblete Rapillon has incorporated elements of Judo and Silat into its empty hand component, as Mena spent some time in both Japan and Indonesia. Although originally composed of thirteen fighting "styles" (techniques or methods), Doblete Rapillon now contains fifty-two.

Training Progressions

Traditionally, Doblete Rapillon included in its curriculum the single stick, double sticks, sword and dagger, and the empty hands. Today, however, the focus of the art is on the single stick and the concurrent use of two twelve-inch pointed daggers, a method known as *arka*.

The first thing students learn on entering the system is footwork, after which various methods and sequences of strikes are taught, which include horizontal, vertical, uppercut, and fanning motions. And while many styles of Arnis incorporate the use of five, seven, and/or twelve angles of attack, Doblete Rapillon has a set of twenty-four strikes in its basic level, thirty-two in its intermediate level, and fifty-four in its advanced level. Interestingly, after the twenty-four strikes are taught in long range, students are then taught a simpler sequence of five strikes, followed by another set of five strikes.

Once this is perfected, the *doblete rapillon larga mano* defensive style is taught, wherein a series of two strikes along the same line or angle of attack are executed in succession, like a propeller.

This is followed by instruction in offensive techniques, methods of closing-the-gap, and blocking. There are thirty-two blocks in the system, each with at least five possible follow-up techniques which, employing the *doblete rapillon* concept, follow the same path of motion. It is believed that by countering in this way, an opponent will be overwhelmed by the continuous heavy blows to the same area, and will thus be unable to counter attack.

Once the core striking, defensive, and counter attack techniques are perfected, various methods of disarming and joint locking are taught, both weapon against weapon and empty hand against weapon. Joint locks are the mechanism through which disarms can be affected in medium and close ranges. When employed, one hand locks and controls the opponent's attacking limb, while the other hand either disarms the weapon or strikes the opponent.

There is no set time frame to learning this art, as students are taught as quickly as they are able to learn and perfect the material at each level. It is not uncommon for a student of

Doblete Rapillon to be introduced to new material every two weeks or so.

While the classical art of Doblete Rapillon was composed of eighteen fighting "styles" or techniques, the so-called modern art encompasses fifty-two. The sequence of the fifty-two styles becomes the general curriculum for learning the system, and are as follows: 1) positions to stepping; 2) defense and directions; 3) defense against direction; 4) defense, retreat, and advance; 5) crucifix or right to left, vice-versa, and horizontal; 6) vertical; 7) vertical and horizontal; 8) butterfly; 9) butterfly and fan; 10) propeller; 11) propeller fan and horizontal; 12) fan and horizontal; 13) letter G to horizontal; 14) whirl or revolve swiftly and vertical, double step forward; 15) three front wheels and horizontal; 16) extra number four; 17) extra number four, uppercut, and vertical; 18) three wheels and vertical; 19) the wheel, reverse, and uppercut; 20) wheel, horizontal, and uppercut; 21) vertical crucifix; 22) star; 23) half moon, double to head, and horizontal; 24) half moon, letter K, and uppercut; 25) propeller, uppercut, and face; 26) butterfly, horizontal, and uppercut; 27) whirl, jump vertical, and horizontal; 28) propeller, back step, advance, head, and horizontal; 29) whirl, side step, ribs, and face; 30) half moon to face and neck; 31) fan, wheel, and uppercut; 32) letter H; 33) half uppercut; 34) fan, uppercut, and wheel; 35) moon, horizontal, propeller, uppercut, and vertical; 36) thrust, retreat, fan, uppercut, head, and face; 37) uppercut left and right, thrust, retreat, face; 38) jab head, uppercut; 39) thrust to eyes, retreat, fan, uppercut, feet, and head; 40) the prayer; 41) wheel, uppercut, and horizontal; 42) half moon, chin, and neck; 43) jab to face, fan to ribs, and uppercut; 44) half moon, vertical, horizontal, uppercut; 45) thrust to neck, uppercut to testicles and head; 46) jab to hand, ribs, and chin; 47) half moon to ribs, vertical, horizontal, and uppercut; 48) thrust to heart, retreat, ribs, vertical, and face; 49) lace, uppercut, fan, horizontal; 50) *rapillon* or rapid motions of all kinds of strokes; 52) general defense and attack of all kinds.

Training Methods

Practitioners of Doblete Rapillon view the fifty-two "styles" in their art as being at once practical and complete, thus requiring few training methods to aid in their effectiveness. In terms of learning and practicing the art's fundamentals, an instructor will demonstrate the techniques, after which students will pair off and practice executing them in turn.

In terms of solo training, beginners practice various sets of pre-arranged forms, containing various combinations of footwork, strikes, and blocks. When students become more advanced, however, these pre-arranged sets are replaced with free-style practice. It is through such free-style practice that skills in visualization and spontaneity are developed. It is believed that this method of practice better prepares the practitioner for sparring and actual combat, as it quickens the mind and hones the reflexes.

Fighting Strategies

While the term Doblete Rapillon is the name of this system, it is also the primary fighting strategy employed therein. The term means "double propellers" and is a method of fighting an opponent in long range, striking with doubled-up, circular strikes along a given angle, one after the other in a succession. In other words, countering with combinations of two continuous strikes along a single circular path, followed by two circu-

lar strikes along another angle, and so on. Thus, when an opponent strikes, the *doblete rapillon* strategy is employed by hitting the opponent's weapon-holding hand with the first strike in the circle, and with the second strike hitting the opponent's head or other vital target.

Timing and control of distance are the key components to applying this art and using it effectively against an opponent. One must be able to maintain his distance while blocking or striking the opponent's hand and then countering with the same weapon, along the same line, in a single motion and in a single moment.

Another key strategy practitioners use is not allowing their opponent to block or even touch their strikes with his weapon or empty hands. It is a method of striking to one location and if the opponent reacts in time, changing the striking angle to hit the opponent elsewhere. This strategy enables practitioners to maintain their attack without interruption, while also acting as a means of feinting and drawing the opponent's guard to one location and then striking in his newly opened area. Practitioners believe that with this strategy, they cannot be disarmed because, after all, one cannot disarm what they cannot grab.

The strategy that perhaps makes Doblete Rapillon Arnis most effective is that of focusing in on the opponent, entering into the art's preferred fighting range, and then launching attacks and counters without pause until the opponent is out of commission.

Free-Sparring

Practitioners of Doblete Rapillon Arnis only spar with the single stick, believing that this is the most practical use of training time, for if one is attacked there is a chance that they will be able to secure at least one object to be used as a weapon. Double sticks and stick and dagger are used for coordination training, and are applied in sparring only if the practitioner has secured the opponent's weapon through a disarm, and are thus holding two weapons.

When engaged in sparring, it is free-style, with no pre-set sequences or rules of engagement. And while an un-padded rattan stick is used and no body armor worn (except for by female students), practitioners do wear a padded glove and a helmet to keep them from the more serious injuries that are unnecessary in training.

Most of all, sparring is viewed in Doblete Rapillon Arnis as a test of skill, stamina, and mental framework, as it trains its practitioners to be able to engage in and withstand fifteen or twenty consecutive minutes of weapons combat.

Grandmaster Ramiro U. Estalilla

11

ESTALILLA KABAROAN ESKRIMA

Ramiro U. Estalilla, Jr., began studying Filipino weapon arts in 1941 during World War II. Kabaroan is attributed to, and so named after, the nobility (Lord Barons) who practiced the art in days past. Estalilla learned the art in Cotabato from his father, Ramiro A, Estalilla, Sr.—who learned it from Eusebio Estalilla, Gregorio Aglipay, and Don Mariano Rigonan—from his uncle, Bernardo Banay, and also from Braulio Roque and Milardo Presas.

Training Progressions

Estalilla Kabaroan Eskrima is a complex and well-structured system that employs the use of single and double weapons, such as the short and long stick *(baston)*, staff *(bangkaw)*, spear *(sibat)*, shield *(kalasag)*, dagger *(daga)*, and sword *(kampilan)*, and the empty hand self-defense translations of their related techniques.

Training is categorized into simple weaponry and compound weaponry. Simple weaponry is divided into *sencilla* (wherein a single weapon is wielded with a single hand) and *bambolla* (wherein a single weapon is wielded with two hands). Practitioners switch back and forth between these methods as necessary during combat. Compound weaponry includes the concurrent use of two weapons, and is divided into weapons of equal length (e.g., double sticks, daggers, or staffs), and weapons of unequal length (e.g., short and long sticks, stick and staff, or shield and spear).

Empty hand techniques are taught inasmuch as they reflect the movements of the sinawali double stick patterns, and include such skills as trapping, releasing from holds, and disarming. However, as Kabaroan is first and foremost a weapons system, skills in unarmed combat are deemed less important.

All beginners to the system are indoctrinated in its underlying mission statement and moral philosophy of teaching and practicing the art "in the context of Philippine history and culture, humanizing the art, civilizing the artist, and refining the system." Students are then introduced to the general lines of strikes, which follow the shape of an octagon, featuring perpendicular, horizontal, and diagonal lines and totaling eight

basic lines of attack. Rather than using a numbering system to identify the strikes, this art names each strike based on its descriptive acronym (i.e., "horlef" for a horizontal strike from the left, and "overlef" for an over-head, diagonal strike from the left). Blocks, in turn, are also so-named after the line of strikes (e.g., a "hor-lef" block after a "horlef" strike). This

109

method of naming techniques removes the often daunting task of memorizing Filipino terms for those who are not so inclined.

Complimenting the eight basic lines of strikes are six types or characteristics of strikes, including chop *(tadtad)*, slash *(pa-iwa)*, thrust *(bagsul)*, butt *(bambu)*, gore *(suag)*, and slam *(barang)*. In addition to executing these six types of strikes along the basic eight lines of the octagon, the perpendicular line as a center point of reference is added, thus making three left side strikes, two main centerline strikes, and three right side strikes. When all of the above are combined, the eight lines and six types total forty-eight different strikes that can be executed along each of three levels, thus becoming a total of 144 strikes.

Once students have a basic understanding of the conceptual nature of strikes and skill in their execution, footwork is introduced—first alone as a warm-up and then in conjunction with the strikes. There are a number of geometric footwork patterns utilized, such as trapezoidal, zigzag, circular, triangular, linear, pivotal, and so on.

The general principle of footwork is to develop hand/foot coordination so that striking reach and power are maximized. To have maximum reach for a right-handed person, for instance, the right foot must be forward. Yet when executing an "underright" (or underhand strike from the right side), a horizontal right, or an overright strike from the right side, the left foot must be forward in order for the right hand to wield the weapon with maximum power and body torque.

Once a basic understanding of striking lines and execution with footwork is gained, sequences of five and twelve strikes are taught. It is these striking combinations that rest at the core of training the appropriate defenses against them. Defensive techniques follow two conceptual methods: *tiradin* (force-to-force blocking then countering) and *todasan* (merging or blending with the force and then countering). By developing these defensive skills in conjunction with the 144 strikes and basic blocks, disarms, and counter disarms, practitioners are able to increase their repertoire manifold.

All strikes are then performed against an opponent, who in turn learns their proper defenses and counters. Disarming techniques follow, of which there are three classes: direct, indirect, and empty-hand. Direct disarming refers to a direct hit to the weapon, the weapon-holding hand, or the side of the head that controls it. Indirect disarms refer to a technique executed with the back-up hand, the weapon hand, or both hands after a successful block and immobilization of the opponent's weapon and/or weapon-hand has been made. Empty hand disarms refer to weaponless techniques with both empty hands, effected either from the onset of the altercation or after the practitioner has been disarmed.

Training then progresses to methods of block, counter, disarm, lock, and then how to counter each of those methods. This is first practiced against the five strike set and then against the twelve strike set. A number of solo and partner training drills are also found throughout the curriculum to further develop skills.

There is a ranking structure used in Estalilla Kabaroan Eskrima based on the Philippine and American education systems. After one year of intensive training, a practitioner may be promoted to a "certified instructor assistant." After two years of training, a practitioner may be promoted to a "certified associate instructor." After four years of dedicated training, a practitioner may be promoted to a "certified bachelor instructor." And after six years, if they are deserving, a practitioner may be awarded the "certified master instructor" certificate.

Training Methods

Training in Estalilla Kabaroan Eskrima is divided into three categories: calisthenic, sportive, and combative. All training is geared to develop the necessary attributes of combat, especially ambidexterity. Ambidexterity is the state or quality of being able to use both hands with equal ease, and one must learn the footwork that makes the left hand and foot do what the right hand and foot can do.

Calisthenic Kabaroan training is primarily intended for physical fitness. It aims to develop rhythm, coordination, alertness, dexterity, speed, strength, and beauty of figure with the ultimate goal of developing a healthy body, mind, and spirit.

Sportive Kabaroan training includes the calisthenic objectives and is geared toward safe, honorable, intramural competition within respective ranks, styles, and schools.

Combative Kabaroan training encompasses the goals of calisthenic and sportive Kabaroan as it anticipates a defense for the honor and safety of the country, of the family, of another person, or of oneself. Within the combative aspect is found three stages of training: demonstration, pre-arranged drills, and free sparring.

Demonstration is based on the so-called "follow the leader" method, wherein the teacher leads the class by demonstration of movements and techniques and students do their best to follow along and mimic the lessons. Such instruction includes the demonstration of forms, strikes, and defenses, movements of head and body, hands and feet, parries and evasions, steps and positions, individually or collectively.

Pre-arranged partner drills involve planned and controlled strikes and defenses that are made in repetition. Two partners face off and engage in an exchange of pre-set strikes and blocks with controlled contact first following the set of five

strikes and then following the set of twelve strikes. While the sequence of strikes and respective limitations of each partner is set for each drill, practitioners may employ either the *tiradin* or *todasan* methods of defense as they wish.

Double sticks are learned and trained in an extended series of sinawali exercises and patterns. These include the three general categories of the system, known as *binaston, binangkaw, bambolia*—with either weapons of equal or unequal length. *Binaston* contains seven levels: level one has ten patterns, level two has twenty-four patterns, level three has twenty-eight patterns, and levels four through ten contain five patterns each. *Binangkaw* and *bambolia* each contain five patterns.

There are also ten pre-arranged solo forms utilized in Estalilla Kabaroan Eskrima. These include series of six strikes, twelve strikes, fifteen strikes, the "alpha twenty-six" form, and the *bambolia* long and short forms. From here, practitioners come to understand the theory of combining the forms to create sequences of their own.

The Kabaroan "abridged fifteen" form contains linear and multi-directional movement, and consists of nine *sencillan* and six *bambolian* strikes.

Practitioners are encouraged to also perform all of the techniques and drills of the system as solo forms, utilizing any combination of strikes, footwork, and blocks in each of the four directions.

Fighting Strategies

The articulated fighting strategies of Estalilla Kabaroan Eskrima are as well thought out as the system itself. When facing an opponent armed with a long weapon, practitioners utilize lateral movement to distract the opponent and keep him from landing a lethal blow. Practitioners also train to be able to deliver strikes while moving at long range with ninety-nine percent accuracy.

Another method unique to this system is that of gripping the weapon in such a way that one can elongate it at will. Since most of the weapons are of greater than thirty inches in length, they are held in their middle, or two-thirds of the way down the shaft, leading the opponent to think he is in medium or close range, and then elongates his weapon to strike the unsuspecting opponent from a different range.

Another strategy when using compound (or multiple) weapons, is to throw one of the weapons at the opponent. This allows the practitioner to land the first, and perhaps only, blow of the altercation, in addition to creating openings in the opponent's guard as he attempts to block the on-coming weapons, and finishing him off with the secondary weapon. The key to effecting this strategy is to only throw the first weapon after the opponent has first wielded his weapon in such a way as to open one of his vital targets. Moreover, this method is only done in medium range, as it is impossible to do so from close range, and too easy for the opponent to block or avoid from long range.

When facing multiple opponents, practitioners will use surprise tactics, such as looking at one opponent but attacking another, or utilizing various methods of faking and feinting to create openings.

Free-Sparring

Free sparring is an important part of skills development in Estalilla Kabaroan Eskrima. After twenty-to-thirty hours of training students are encouraged to begin pitting their skills against

their classmates in a controlled manner, at first using only the first five lines of strikes. There are two basic methods for developing free sparring skills: free style solo and free style bout.

Free style solo sparring is a method in which the individual player demonstrates forms, strikes, and defenses in the air against an imaginary opponent. Emphasis here is on artistic representation of technique and refinement of execution in the performance of martial art dance. This method is a preliminary one and is used to develop skills in visualization and spontaneous technique combinations.

The free style bout, conversely, find two practitioners engage in a spontaneous exchange of techniques, each trying to hit the other. In this method, practitioners display highly-controlled strikes and defenses, but draw from their individual resources, from their wealth of knowledge, skills, training, and experience. It is optional for the students to wear protective armor. For safety purposes, when not wearing armor, the power of strikes is held back and contact is generally light.

Today, under controlled practices, Estalilla Kabaroan Eskrima is a very safe endeavor. Under guided instructions and controlled practices, the art'uses not only light rattan sticks and wooden swords, but also foam-padded plastic or wooden sticks in lieu of bladed weapons for extended periods of training.

Underlying the system at every level, however, is the following moral philosophy: "No matter how deadly your art and style may be, you must control your strikes within the sphere of good motives against the background of peaceful intentions."

Gat Puno Abondio Baet

12

GARIMOT ARNIS

The Garimot Arnis system was developed by Abondio "Garimot" Baet in 1993, after synthesizing the essence of what he learned from various masters in the province of Laguna, Philippines. These include: the respective Largo Mano systems of Rufino "Pining" Absin, Jose Dimasaka and Myrna Cadang; the Sobrada Herada system of Tomas Cagayat; the Largo Mano de Abaniko system of Clemente Afunggol; the Herada Corto de Abaniko system of Indo Afunggol; the Sobrada de San Miguel system of Juan Alejandro Cacaos and Juan Ladiana; and the Herada Corto de Payong system of Totoy Acuno.

Training Progressions

Training in Garimot Arnis consists of eight categories, based on the following weapons: single stick *(solo brokil)*, double sticks *(doble brokil)*, stick and dagger *(tabak at balaraw)*, knife *(balisong)*, walking cane *(tunkod)*, spear *(sibat)*, headband or handkerchief *(panyo)*, and belt *(bigkis)*.

The art's training curriculum is based on a set of progressive stages, beginning concurrently with the single stick and double sticks. Each stage is based on weapon training and is denoted by a particular sash color *(bigkis)* and a designated time in rank.

The beginning student *(bagito)* wears a yellow sash, designating the stage of "challenges." Within this rank there are three degrees of promotion, each requiring a minimum time in rank of three months. The first degree *(antas isa)* consists of the five angles of attack *(cinco tero),* five basic footwork movements, methods of gripping the stick, five fighting stances, five blocking techniques, and the first form known as *moro moro batalya isa,* which is performed solo and with a partner. The second degree *(antas dalawa)* consists of basic blocks and counters, the first and second theories of disarming, two additional *moro-moro batalya* forms, and two *abaniko* (fanning) double stick methods. The third degree *(antas tatlo)* consists of long range *(largo mano)* counters, the third and fourth theories of disarming, the fourth and fifth *moro moro batalya* forms, two *sinawali* (weaving) double stick methods, basic knife fighting movements and their application.

The intermediate student *(dugong kayumangi)* wears a brown sash with red trim, designating the stage of "loyalty." Within this rank there are also three degrees of promotion, each requiring a minimum time in rank of six months. The first degree consists of the seven ways of attack *(siete colores),* seven related blocks and counters, the third lock and disarming theory, the sixth and seventh *moro moro batalya* forms, the third *abaniko* and *sinawali* double stick methods, basic stick and dagger movements, and the *sambutan* knife fighting techniques. The second degree consists of the fourth disarming theory, the seventh and eighth *moro-moro batalya* forms, the fourth *abaniko* and *sinawali* double stick methods, and the *tabuyan* knife fighting techniques. The third degree consists of the ninth and tenth *moro-moro batalya* forms, long range *(largo*

mano), medium range *(herada),* and close range *(corto)* single stick applications, the fifth *abaniko* and *sinawali* double stick methods, empty hand weaving *(sulsihan)* and chained or linked *(cadena de mano)* movements, and the *baliktaran* knife fighting techniques.

The senior student *(dugong maharlika)* wears a black sash with red trim, designating the stages of "mastery." Within this level, there are a total of ten degrees. Teachers are called *guro,* and hold the ranks of *batikan* (first through fifth degrees), with a time in rank requirement of one year in the first two

degrees, two years in the third and fourth degrees, and three years in the fifth degree. Head teachers are called *punong guro,* and hold the rank of *gat* (sixth through tenth degrees), with a time in rank requirement of five years per degree. The grand-master is called *gat puno,* and is the only possessor of the twelfth degree, which is two ranks above the highest student.

Training Methods

There are a number of empty hand and weapon training methods utilized in Garimot Arnis, from solo repetition of movements to two-person pre-arranged and free form drills.

In a general sense, Garimot Arnis is a composite of the techniques and methods of three core styles: Cinco Tero, Siete Colores, and Doce Pares (of Laguna, not Cebu). Cinco Tero consists of five footwork maneuvers, five strikes, five blocks, five counters, five disarms, and so on. Siete Colores consists of seven footwork maneuvers, seven strikes, seven blocks, seven counters, seven disarms, and so on. And Doce Pares consists of twelve footwork maneuvers, twelve strikes, twelve blocks, twelve counters, twelve disarms, and so on. Within these methods, Garimot Arnis practitioners learn the art through repetition of movements and techniques by themselves and with partners.

In addition to these three core systems of training, Garimot Arnis has adopted the *batalya* or fighting dances from the classic Filipino *moro-moro* and *komedya* stage plays. These forms are spread out over the curriculum, and are performed solo and with a partner. It is through these forms that practitioners first learn and perfect fighting movements and sequences on their own and then practice their intended applications with a partner.

There is also a set of seven two-man drills for developing skills in knife fighting known as *laban tulisan,* or fighting points. These drills develop in practitioners stamina, reflexes, hand/eye coordination, proper timing, and the self-confidence necessary to obtain a natural reaction to any situation.

Fighting Strategies

The fighting strategies of Garimot Arnis are based on the theory of a "body box"—or vicinity in which the body is protected at long, medium, and close ranges. It is the range in which one finds himself, the weapon he and his opponent possess, and the techniques applicable therein that determine the strategy used.

In long range *(largo mano)*, meticulous measured angles, footwork, body mechanics, and weapon power are used to take advantage of the opponent, regardless of the length of weapons being used.

In medium range *(herada)*, various techniques of parrying, passing, blocking, and countering with the weapons are utilized.

In close range *(corto mano)*, the strategic concepts of *abaniko* (fanning motions), *rendondo* (circling motions), and *punyo* (grip-end thrusting) are utilized. Once inside the *corto* range, practitioners attempt to control their "body box" in such a way as to use correct body mechanics to stop the power of an opponent's blows and effectively deliver a counter attack with minimum effort.

As most people tend to want to "take out" their opponent as early as possible, practitioners of Garimot Arnis prefer to wait for their opponent's attack, to then find their openings and use their own techniques against them. This is a philosophy which has time and again proven effective, as the opponent's aggression is absorbed and their techniques "reversed" in a way wherein the attacker must then defend against his own attack. In other words, a strong defense is the best offense.

Free-Sparring

Free-sparring is a core component of Garimot Arnis, and is reserved for practitioners at the intermediate and advanced levels. Free-sparring is confined to stick fighting and is separated into three types: single stick, double sticks, and concurrent use of one long and one short stick.

While beginners do not engage in sparring, they observe matches between advanced students in an effort to acquire pointers, learn what mistakes are to be avoided, and discover which counters work best against which types of attacks.

Sparring in the intermediate and advanced levels is strong and develops stamina, quick reactions, speed, accuracy, and superb hand/eye coordination. The notion of "fair play" is put to use, as practitioners are expected to conduct themselves accordingly, with etiquette requiring combatants to duly acknowledge all hits against themselves.

Grandmaster Leo Giron

13

GIRON ARNIS ESCRIMA

Leovigildo M. Giron began studying Escrima in 1922. In Pangasinan he studied the Cabaroan (long range) style under Benito Junio and the Cadaanan (close range) style under Julian Bundoc. In Bayambang he studied the Macabebe Sinawali (double stick) style under Fructuso Junio. And while living in Meridian, California in 1929, he studied Arnis and Escrima under Flaviano Vergara. The most important thing Giron extracted from Vergara was the need to develop his own system that would effectively bridge the gap between the three systems he had previously learned. It was then that Giron developed his own style of Arnis he termed *estilo de fondo* (planted position) and then created the Bahala Na system of Filipino martial arts. This system was honed during Giron's jungle warfare action in World War II, and is now headed by Antonio Somera, its current grandmaster.

Training Progressions

The Giron Arnis Escrima system is composed of twenty individual methods of play. The term "method" is used here rather than style or technique, as these methods are sometimes techniques, sometimes concepts, sometimes strategies. The twenty methods are represented on the *abanico del maestro* (fan of the master), which is composed of twenty ribs beginning with *estilo de fondo* (planted close range combat) and ending with *larga mano* (long range combat). In essence, the fan represents the training progressions and fighting methods of Giron's system, wherein there are eighteen methods that must be developed and perfected for a student to master all the strategies and transitions that exist between the extreme close and long ranges of combat.

Since most altercations begin in close proximity to an opponent, the *de fondo* style is the first method of defense taught to students. It takes approximately 200 hours of training, or two years time, for one to develop a strong foundation and understanding of this method. During the next two years students are required to learn the following additional nine methods: *estilo abanico* (fanning method), *estilo sonkete* (thrusting method), *estilo retirada* (retreating method), *combate adentro* (in-fighting method), *estilo Macabebe* (two stick method), *candena de mano* (empty hand method), *escapo* (evading method), *fondo fuerte* (anchoring method), and *larga mano* (long range method).

Many more elements are needed to complete this stage of training, including: salutation, with and without a weapon; the understanding and delivery of the twelve angles of attack; and the theories of parrying, deflecting, evading, and hand checking. During this time practitioners are also required to learn the historical and cultural aspect of the arts. In addition, throughout the course of their training students are taught to

train their mind (to come to understand the spiritual components), their heart (to persevere, tolerate, forgive, love, embrace fidelity, and have compassion), and their body (to develop endurance, strength, and stamina).

The remaining ten methods of the system (i.e., *estilo abierta, estilo de salon, estilo elastico, contra compas, estilo redonda, tero grave, tero pisada, media media, estilo bolante,* and *miscla contras*) are reserved for those truly dedicated to furthering their knowledge of and mastering Giron Arnis Escrima. In addition to these ten methods, practitioners must develop an understanding of the four basic distances associated with each method and their relation to an opponent. These distances are: *corto* (close range), *tersia* (one-third distance), *media* (one-half distance), and *larga* (long range).

Training Methods

Giron Arnis Escrima incorporates many different partner training drills to develop the necessary skills of reacting to an alive and reacting opponent. The drills are structured into three categories, each focusing on one of the three combat ranges.

The first drill is known as the *corto* or close range drill, and finds two partners, one as attacker and one as defender, facing each other in close proximity. The attacker is armed with a weapon of his choosing; the defender is unarmed. At the basic level, the attacker will repeatedly strike the defender with angles one and two. As the strikes near, the defender will use his left hand to parry the weapon-holding hand, repositioning it to his right side, maintaining contact and pressure to the attacker's weapon hand throughout. In order to avoid being struck by the on-coming weapon, the defender must step directly back with his right foot. From here, the attacker delivers strike number two, at which time the defender must parry the attacker's arm to his left side. The defender will also retreat with his left foot in order to keep from being struck by the weapon. The defender will always retreat with the leg in which the attacker's weapon will be positioned.

This drill can be preformed with the defender retreating, advancing, or maneuvering in a circle around the attacker. The drill can also be preformed using all of the attacking angles, not just being limited to the first two.

The *media* drill is learned only after a student has perfected the defensive movements developed in the *corto* drill, as this is a counter-for-counter or preparatory sparing drill. Using angles one and two, the defender is limited to utilizing the outside, inside, and roof blocks and their counters, all from a right foot lead.

The drill begins with the attacker delivering a number one strike. The defender counters the strike with an outside block and immediately counters with a number one strike of his own. The attacker now becomes the defender, blocking with a roof block and returning a number two strike. The defender counters this with an inside block and returns a number two strike of his own.

This exchange continues until the practitioners have reviewed all the blocks they have learned against angles one and two. In isolated cases, the participants can change their footwork to better avoid or deliver a strike, but must reposition back to the right foot lead. Students should not try to move around too much during the drill, as this will cause fatigue and the terrain may play a part in disturbing the flow, and the players may invite injury. The drill should also be performed on different elevations. As the practitioner's skill advances, the speed of the exchange will increase, and the type, weight, and length of weapons employed can change.

The third primary drill is known as the *larga* or long range drill, and is performed with both partners (one attacker and the other defender) using weapons of at least thirty-two inches. They begin in a right foot lead, ensuring that their foot is pointing in the direction of their target, while not restricting stretching ability. And while striking angles can change, in the beginning levels practitioners face each other directly in long range. The attacker will strike at the defender along the *cinco tero* (five strikes), which the defender will react to as follows: As the attacker initiates the number one strike, the defender leans back to avoid it and counters by stretching forward and delivering a number one strike in return. As the attacker initiates the number two strike, the defender leans back to avoid it and counters by stretching forward and delivering a number two strike in return. And so on through the five strikes. The practitioners then switch roles and repeat.

This drill increases the stretching ability and speed necessary to fight effectively from long range. In addition, wielding a long and heavy weapon increases upper body strength and lower body flexibility and conditioning. At advanced levels, this drill is preformed at different heights, including while standing on benches, tables, and embankments.

Fighting Strategies

The fighting strategies of Giron Arnis Escrima are inherent in the system's twenty methods, each representing a specific method of attack, defense, movement, and so on.

The first is *estilo de fondo,* a method wherein the practitioner keeps a closed guard and fights in close range while maintaining solid footing. This is the foundation of the Giron system.

The second is *estilo de abanico,* which is a fanning style wherein blocking and striking are done in a side-to-side motion (to look like an open fan). It is a fast and dynamic method of parrying and striking with the weapon on two or more lines of attack.

The third is *estilo abierta,* which is a method of fighting from an open guard position. This method finds the practitioner luring the opponent's attack to a specific area, which is then easily countered.

The fourth is *estilo de salon,* which employs fast, deceptive, and aggressive foot maneuvering and body repositioning to outflank the opponent.

The fifth is *estilo sonkete,* which employs thrusts to areas of an opponent's body that may otherwise be guarded against swinging-type blows. It's techniques are similar to those found in Western foil fencing.

The sixth is *estilo retirada,* which is a retreating method wherein an opponent is lured into overextending his attack, as the blow nears, the practi-

tioner moves back and strikes the opponent's now over-exposed body.

The seventh is *estilo elastico,* which stretches the body back and forth between close and long ranges as needed to defend or attack. In essence, it successfully employs the extreme ranges while the practitioner remains in one place to throw-off an opponent's depth perception to then catch him off-guard.

The eighth is *fondo fuerte,* which finds the practitioner holding his ground and waiting for the opponent to attack first, at which time he counters to the opponent's open area. It is often held that he who moves first, loses.

The ninth is *contra compas,* which is a method of employing broken rhythm and off-beat timing to evade, off-balance, and attack an opponent.

The tenth is *estilo redonda,* which is a circular style of striking and blocking from front to back, side to side, and vertical to horizontal.

The eleventh is *combate adentro,* which is a method of fighting at close range.

The twelfth is *tero grave,* which teaches the most vulnerable and deadly places on the body to counter strike in order to maim or kill an opponent.

The thirteenth is *estilo Macabebe,* which is the double stick Sinawali style of the Macabebe people. This method employs two sticks concurrently, using one to block and the other to strike, or both sticks to first block and then counter.

The fourteenth is *tero pisada,* which is a method of holding one stick with both hands. This method is necessary when facing an opponent who is wielding a much larger or heavier weapon.

The fifteenth is *media media,* which means half-half and refers to mid range beats of striking. It is a method employed to probe or feel-out an opponent's style.

The sixteenth is *cadena de mano,* which is are unarmed methods of defending, blocking, locking, and/or disarming armed or unarmed opponents.

The seventeenth is *escapo,* wherein hand and foot movements are synchronized to allow an armed or unarmed opponent to effectively escape or maneuver around an attacking, weapon-wielding opponent.

The eighteenth is *estilo Bolante,* which consists of methods of fighting in doorways and narrow halls or alleyways where wide swinging or maneuvering are impossible.

The nineteenth is *miscla contras,* which employs methods of fighting multiple opponents and using everything in your means to survive.

The twentieth and final fighting strategy is *larga mano.* This is the so-called "bread and butter" of the Giron system, as it is at once the easiest to employ and the most difficult to defend against. It is a strategy of directly striking the opponent's attacking arm from long range, while employing body shifting to be out of the attacker's range.

As far as an underlying combative strategy used in Giron Arnis Escrima, it is simple: Stay alive at all costs, chose targets wisely, and use no wasted movements.

Free-Sparring

Free sparing in Giron Arnis Escrima is only undertaken by students who have first learned the necessary and requisite defenses against the first five angles of *estilo de fondo.* Sparring makes use of counter striking and counter blocking between combatants. The theory of introductory levels is to acquaint the combatants with the path of the weapon, where it is expected to travel and land, and too use the *de fondo* style of blocking and striking. For the more advanced students, or after the practitioners are comfortable with the rhythm and movements of *estilo de fondo,* any of the other nineteen strategic methods of play may be employed.

As there are no pre-set patterns in Giron free sparing, it is a great way to improve weapon/eye coordination with body and foot movements. What does remain consistent, however, is the sequence of play: strike-counter, block-counter, strike-counter, block-counter, and so on, regardless of block or counter striking angle employed.

While practitioners train in the Giron system for self-defense and sport, they must also train in and embrace the art of sportsmanship and develop respect and compassion for their fellow man and God. When all is said and done, training in Giron Arnis Escrima is done for the sake of self-preservation and to insure the legacy of the forefathers who handed down their art down to the current generations.

Guro Chris Kent

14

JKD/KALI

The Filipino martial art perpetuated by Dan Inosanto and his students is generically known as "Kali," and is grounded in elements of the respective systems of Floro Villabrille, Juanito LaCoste, Leo Giron, Angel Cabales, Lucky Lucaylucay, Jack Santos, Sam Tendencia, Gilbert Tenio, Dionisio Cañete, Ciricao Cañete, and Edgar Sulate, among others.

As most practitioners of "Kali" also follow Bruce Lee's art and philosophy of Jeet Kune Do, there is much cross-training in other (non-Filipino) systems. Thus, practitioners of Kali prefer not to attach "limiting" labels or names to their expression of the Filipino martial arts, preferring instead to grab concepts and techniques from whichever source and integrate them into their expression of the arts. However, over the years a common training progression and teaching method has developed among practitioners of Inosanto's method, and the term JKD/Kali (or the Jeet Kune Do expression of the Filipino martial arts) has become a term to refer to it.

While the basic techniques and drills of JKD/Kali vary little amongst practitioners of this art, each instructor reflects on their own experience and adjusts the curriculum and training to fit their needs and the needs of their students. The following is a presentation of JKD/Kali as expressed and perpetuated by Chris Kent, one of Inosanto's senior students.

Training Progressions

In his attempt to be a well-rounded Kali teacher, Kent's curriculum includes single stick, single sword, double sticks, double swords, stick and dagger, sword and dagger, single and double dagger, staff, spear, and the empty hands. This well-rounded approach offers practitioners the ability to develop a functional working knowledge of all types of weapons. Over time, students are drawn to their particular area(s) of interest in the art. Some are drawn more to the single stick, others to the double sticks, and still others to the knife. However, they are taught to understand the particular characteristics of each type of weapon and how to use them in order to be prepared for any encounter.

Kent takes a very "JKD" approach to teaching the Filipino fighting arts. He has a progressive training program laid out for each of the various categories, taking students from "point A"—where they know nothing or very little about the weapons and their uses—to "point Z"—where they have developed the ability to use the weapons not only with both right and left hands, but against all types of weapons and in long, medium, and close ranges. The JKD/Kali training program is designed like the academic curriculum of a school, in which each succeeding learning period builds upon the previous one. Like learning mathematics, you learn basic addition and subtraction before algebra, geometry, and other advanced methods.

Beginners generally start their training with both single stick and double sticks in order to give them a solid foundation in

the basics. The empty hand dimension is taught simultaneously with the stick training so students can immediately see the relationship between armed and unarmed combat. From there, students progress to using stick and dagger, sword and dagger, and single and double knife, after which longer weapons such as the staff and spear are introduced.

For a student to progress from one level of instruction to another really depends upon the individual. The JKD/Kali curriculum is not such that a student has to perfect everything in one category, or have perfect form in what they do before they're able move on to another area. For instance, a thorough understanding of the single stick is not a prerequisite to learning the stick and dagger, or the *sumbrada* flow drill. However, a functional, working knowledge of the use of the single stick is a must. Thus, whereas one person may learn the material in six months, another person might take a year or more.

Training Methods

While each teacher of JKD/Kali has their own focus, the fundamental training, techniques, and drills are generally consistent between them. Two of the most important training methods Kent uses are Angel Cabales' *sumbrada* (counter-for-counter drill) and Floro Villabrille's *numerado* (by-the-numbers drill). If done properly, both drills develop in students reflexes, timing, and a sense of distance. Moreover, and perhaps a result of their vast cross-training, JKD/Kali practitioners practice their drills with varying focus at different times. For instance, sometimes they'll practice *numerado* using circling footwork, and other times using retreating footwork. Sometimes they will practice *sumbrada* using footwork and body angulation, while at other times they'll stand directly in front of their opponent and only use "replace-step" footwork.

After these two drills have been trained significantly, students move on to "free-lance" sparring with protective equipment. This develops in students the ability to function under pressure in a combative situation.

While JKD/Kali does not embrace the use of pre-arranged solo forms, they do practice a kind of "shadow boxing" they call *carenza*. While shadowboxing, a student may choose to isolate and work on one particular thing, such as basic deflections, or choose to concentrate on fighting only at long-range. They may visualize that they are fighting a single opponent or several opponents at once. In so doing, they are literally creating their own "free-lance" forms. This method of solo training does much to develop a student's capacity to visualize their attacks and counters while training their minds.

Fighting Strategies

True to the philosophy of Jeet Kune Do, practitioners of JKD/Kali believe that the greatest quality a martial artist can possess is adaptability. One of the primary goals of the JKD/Kali teacher is to develop in their students the ability to pick up any type of weapon and use it efficiently at any given range. In other words, they come to understand the particular characteristics of a weapon and how best to use it. For example, a heavy, long stick can not be used in the same way as a short, light stick.

In addition to adaptability, there are six primary strategies used in JKD/Kali. The first is an understanding and use of the three primary ranges of combat. These deal with the principle that a combative situation can only take place in long range, medium range, or close range.

The second is the use of nine basic angles of attack. This deals with the principle that any attack will travel either on a diagonal downward, diagonal upward, horizontal, vertical, or thrusting line. Thus, learning to defend against a strike's angle of trajectory is more efficient than trying to memorize specific defenses against every conceivable type of attack.

The third principle is that of the "parry-safety check-killing blow" defensive combination. In this scheme, the parry is an initial motion that deflects the attacker's strike. The safety check is the motion that controls or holds the attacker's striking hand in place after his attack has been deflected. The so-called killing blow is the counter-strike. Sometimes, however, the killing blow can also serve as the parry and/or safety check.

The fourth principle is that of "zoning and body angulation." Zoning involves imagining a circle encompassing an opponent, and breaking it down into 180-degree and ninety-degree sections or "zones." The idea is to move to a

zone that offers the greatest safety while at the same time putting the opponent in a less advantageous position. For example, instead of remaining directly in front an opponent where he can effectively use both of his arms and legs to attack, practitioners move to a position on either his left or right side, wherein they can effectively limit his use of one side of his body. Body angulation involves shifting the body either by ducking or angling beneath blows so that they miss, leaving the practitioner in a good position from which to counter.

The fifth principle is known as "zero pressure," or maneuvering to the place where the opponent's strike holds the least power. For instance, one can move forward and "jam" a blow before it has time to gain its momentum, or move with the blow to decrease its momentum. This principle goes hand-in-hand with the principle of zoning.

The sixth principle is known as "defanging the snake," wherein the opponent's weapon hand is considered the snake's fangs. By the practitioner striking the opponent's hand with his weapon and taking it out of commission, the opponent's ability to harm him is effectively removed.

Free-Sparring

Since Bruce Lee's Jeet Kune Do is primarily about fighting, by extension JKD/Kali is also ultimately concerned with free-sparring. After the requisite basics and drills have been learned well, practitioners put on protective gear and go at it. Sometimes they'll use a padded competition style stick, and at other times they'll use a rattan stick or staff. Regardless of how much padding students wear, they will always match their skills against opponent's wielding a variety of weapons. Thus, they learn the strengths and weaknesses of, say, the single stick against the staff or the double sticks.

To be honest about one's skills and to have the ability to employ the art in a realistic setting is the goal of JKD/Kali, and by wearing protective gear practitioners can feel when they have been hit, without becoming crippled. Realism without injury is the key.

Grandmaster Antonio Ilustrisimo

15

KALIS ILUSTRISIMO

The art of Kalis Ilustrisimo encompasses the ancient sword techniques of the southern Philippines, the classical sword and dagger methods of the central Philippines, and the contemporary systematization and teaching structure of the northern Philippines. While the Ilustrisimo family art can be traced back five generations in the Ilustrisimo clan, the art of the late Antonio Ilustrisimo is different from the others as a result of his instruction under Pedro Cortez and his experiences in numerous challenge and death matches. More importantly, Kalis Ilustrisimo can be viewed as a microcosm of the Filipino arts in general, as it continually evolves to suite the times and needs of its practitioners.

Training Progressions

Although based in sword techniques, Kalis Ilustrisimo is a complete weapon-based art that encompasses many types and classifications of weapons. Regarding edged weapons, the art utilizes the *barong, kris, itak, pinute, bolo,* and *daga.* Regarding impact weapons, the art utilizes the short stick, long stick, and staff. Regarding flexible weapons, the art utilizes the rope, chain, and handkerchief. Regarding the empty hands, the art utilizes parrying, locking, striking, and disarming techniques against weapons and the empty hands.

In terms of weapon use, Kalis Ilustrisimo employs them solo and in pairs, with both one and two hands. Moreover, every technique in the system is such that it can be adapted to various edged, impact, and anatomical weapons—with appropriate adjustments made in timing and positioning, not to mention proper training. As such, Kalis Ilustrisimo is compact in terms of number of pre-set techniques, but comprehensive in terms of employing those techniques in a variety of settings and with a variety of weapons. In essence, the art favors direct striking and disabling, and has no time for showmanship, excessive movement, or lock and control techniques that don't put an immediate end to an altercation.

While there is traditionally no specific progression to learning Kalis Ilustrisimo, the late Antonio Ilustrisimo held that training should begin with the double sticks. By training with two weapons of equal length from the onset, students can concurrently develop skills in both their left and right hands. Be this as it may, in keeping with current trends and expectations, new students of Kalis Ilustrisimo are first taught how to hold and swing the single stick while stationary, and then while moving along various footwork patterns.

As a general guideline, the art is taught with two categories of techniques: defensive counters and defensive follow-up strikes. Basic counter techniques include *estrella* (star-shaped), *cruzada* (cross-shaped), *pluma* (pen-shaped) maneuvers, while follow-ups include *rompida* (up and down), *planchada* (sideways), and *ocho-ocho* (figure eight) maneuvers, among others.

After a level of skill is attained in applying these maneuvers against a cooperative opponent attacking with single, pre-set

strikes, the attacker begins striking spontaneously and the defender responds naturally. It is in this free-flow training that students develop their correct and spontaneous reactions without preliminary thought or hesitation—a skill necessary to employ the art in actual life-and-death situations.

From the single stick students move on to double sticks, and then to either staff, sword, stick and dagger, sword and dagger, or the empty hands, depending on their preference and the teacher's judgement.

Training Methods

Since Kalis Ilustrisimo is a practical and pragmatic art, it only utilizes a few training drills. Nonetheless, these drills develop the students' coordination, speed, timing, distancing, power, conditioning, and an unwavering mind-set—the primary attributes necessary to apply the art.

To develop coordination, the double sticks are twirled in various combinations of upward, downward, and sideways strikes. Training in sword and dagger also develops coordina-

tion, in addition to timing and body mechanics, as the sword and dagger are maneuvered in such a way that they are intersect without touching.

To develop impact power, practitioners strike a rubber car tire mounted from a wall or hung from the ceiling at full force and speed for various lengths of time. In addition to developing power in strikes from all angles, the tire target also develops proper body mechanics, which of course leads to stronger blows.

Timing, coordination, reflexes, and distancing are concurrently developed through a free-flow drill known as *cuatro cantos* (four count). This drill is the cornerstone of training and finds one partner striking while the other partner responds and counters. The drill is first practiced with the single stick in a pattern and later with the attacker striking at random, along any angle. The drill is also practiced with double sticks, stick and dagger, and staff.

To develop a sense of spatial relationship and timing when facing an opponent, practitioners of Kalis Ilustrisimo engage in what they refer to as "target practice." This is limited-target, padded-stick sparring wherein since the targets are known to both opponents ahead of time and are the same (e.g., the

weapon-holding hand), only the practitioner with superior timing and distancing will be able to strike his opponent without himself being struck in the process.

Fighting Strategies

Since the late Antonio Ilustrisimo was a true swordsman—as opposed to merely a stick fighter—the principles and strategies found in his art are those that allow practitioners to survive actual bladed encounters. Unlike stick fighting, dueling with swords offers no forgiveness—a mistake in timing or reaction does not lead to a bruised or broken arm, but a severed limb or instant death.

There exists seven essential principles in Kalis Ilustrisimo that effect the art's techniques, they are: 1) keep calm and relaxed; 2) know your distance; 3) use the shortest path for your trajectory; 4) put the weight of your body behind your strikes; 5) guide the opponent's force rather than meeting it; 6) be an honest and good man, free of guilt and clear of mind and conscience; and 7) know when to break the rules.

In addition to these seven principles, practitioners of Kalis Ilustrisimo know that one cannot effectively employ principles without proper strategies. Thus, from his vast fighting experience, Antonio Ilustrisimo personified and realized seven key strategies for employing his art.

First, move suddenly, precisely, and without delay. In other words, do not waste time awaiting your opponent's strike to block it and then counter. Strike at the first sign of weakness in your opponent, and do so with precision and suddenness so he will have no recourse.

Second, strike directly from the current position of the weapon, without first chambering the blow. If you first chamber your arm to "wind up" your strike, you not only increase the distance your strike must travel to reach its target (thus slowing the blow), but give your opponent an indication that you are striking (thus losing the element of surprise and allowing him to effectively counter).

Third, rather than employing a force-to-force block and then counter maneuver (a two-count method), use precise angling to slip your opponent's blow while striking directly, or redirect his force and counter in the newly opened area. Aside from being too slow, force-to-force blocks only work against a weaker opponent.

Fourth, flank your opponent by moving around him in ninety-degree increments, thus being in a position to strike him while his vulnerable targets are exposed to you.

Fifth, use feinting techniques, known as *enganyo,* to draw your opponent's attack and counter to his unprotected area. Feints are one of the key strategies used in weapons combat to open an otherwise guarded opponent.

Sixth, when facing multiple opponents, keep one foot planted while the other maneuvers you in the eight directions while swinging your weapon in circular motions, keeping the practitioner protected at all times. This will allow the practitioner to maneuver around his opponents and avoid their strikes without giving up his ground.

Seventh, if all else fails, be a fraction of a second faster than your opponent. This last strategy is more concerned with employing properly developed timing, distancing, and footwork than it is with speed alone, as precise timing can often overcome a faster opponent.

Free-Sparring

The goal of Kalis Ilustrisimo training is to develop in its practitioners superior skills in being able to apply their art in realistic encounters. This means not only against other stick fighters in the confines of competition and the spontaneity of anything-goes challenge matches, but also against the often armed criminal element in the unforgiving streets of Manila, and indeed the inner cities around the world.

It is with this in mind, that while practitioners of Kalis Ilustrisimo don headgear and protective equipment to engage one another in full-contact stick fighting matches, they also employ methods of controlled sparring with no padding, and utilize realistic free-flowing drills with sharp bladed weapons.

Grandmaster Omichael del Rosario

16

Kalis Kalis ng Tinagalogan

According to oral tradition, the art of Kalis Kalis ng Tinagalogan is said to be "ancient" with very rich "psycho-los-ophy-legends," wisdom, and principles that date back to the Brahmin Caste of The Sri Visayan Caelandran Kings of Sumatra (600s), Borobudur (800s), Borneo (1200s), and finally to Kalibo (Aklan) and the legendary Princess Urduja of Luzon (early 1300s).

After studying Aikido and Okinawa-te as a child, Kalis Kalis ng Tinagalogan heir, Omichael L. delRosario (called "Guro Omikl D." by his students and Sometimes "Yoda" by others), found they didn't work for him. It was while in the U.S. Navy in 1971 that he met Pinaka Punong Guro Ren Ni (*aka* Master Rey), where he learned "the truth." It was during this training that Guro Omikl was brought into the "secret magical circle" of the system, thus learning all its most revered weapons (sticks, swords, knives), empty hand skills (striking, trapping, sweeping, grappling, wrestling), meditation and philosophy *(diyan-diyan),* and how to write in the ancient *agana* script called *baybayin* by the Tinagalogan.

Training Progressions

Training in Kalis Kalis ng Tinagalogan begins with weapon techniques from long range, proceeds to single weapon and empty-hand striking and trapping in medium range, then to close range grappling, and finally to ground grappling. Within each fighting range is found a sub-system of combat. These form the stages of learning the art and, when combined, constitute the entire Kalis Kalis ng Tinagalogan system.

Training begins with the weapon system known as Kalis Silak. And while practitioners do most of their day-to-day training with sticks. Rather than looking to sticks as blunt weapons, they view them as a simulation of a chopping weapon such as the *kampilan* (dual-pointed sword) for use in *layo* (long range), as a simulation of a stabbing weapon such as the *kalis* (wavy blade sword) for use in *lapit* (medium range), and as a simulation of a slicing weapon such as the *barong* (leaf-shaped sword) for use in *dikit* (close range). In general, however, Kalis Silak techniques and methods are considered *layo,* or techniques best utilized in long range.

The next stage of training is Singkaw Kuntaw, wherein one learns techniques of a single weapon while leaving the other hand unencumbered for trapping *(singkaw)*, pushing/pulling *(tapik-tapik)*, and striking *(hataw)*. Techniques of Singkaw Kuntaw are best utilized in *lapit* or medium range.

From here, students progress to Agaw Patid Buno, or methods of "snatch, trip, and kill." Techniques in this category include *dumog* (overwhelming methods), *gunting* (scissors movements), and *buno* (the application of triangle, weight, and weakness-points leveraging and manipulation principles). Techniques in this category are best utilized in *dikit,* or close range.

The final stage of training is known as Musang Dumog, which encompasses the overwhelming techniques of the *cavet kutching* (wild cat). Such techniques are utilized in *yakap* (grappling) range, and are the necessary but often overlooked follow-up defensive techniques to be employed while on the ground.

Classes in Kalis Kalis ng Tinagalogan run approximately two hours in length. The first hour is dedicated to Kalis Sikak weapons training while the second half is dedicated to the combination of empty hand striking and grappling skills known collectively as Singkaw Buno Dumog.

While there is a basic progression to the ranges, weapons, and techniques students move through, there is no definitive ranking structure, as such is believed to be deceptive. As an example, there are students who train for four years and still move like a beginner, and there are students who perfect their applications in only a short period of time. Thus, rank based on time alone is viewed as absurd, and so it is based on the acronym RASA: Rank belongs to Age (one who is older is called *kuya*), Seniority (one who has been taking lessons longer), Accessibility (one who is accessible to everyone for advice, tutoring, and brotherhood). Thus, respect, more so than rank, is a focal point of practitioner interaction and socialization. Students are taught to demand respect only out of themselves toward others.

For the few students who prove themselves worthy in any number of ways, the master of Kalis Kalis ng Tinagalogan, in this case Guro Omikl D., will invite and initiate them into "the secret magic circle," wherein the most revered and sacred teachings of this art are passed on.

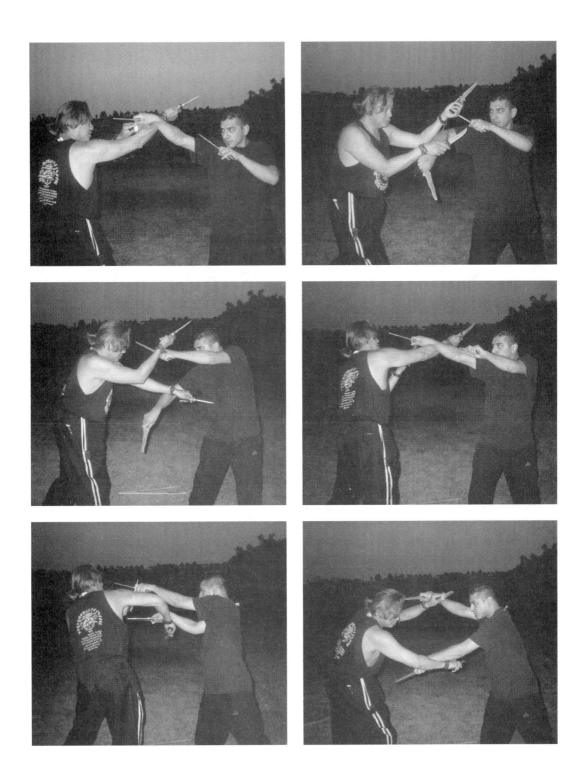

165

Training Methods

There are no pre-arranged training methods employed in Kalis Kalis ng Tinagalogan. It is believed that such things as pre-set solo or partner forms are the domain of other Asian arts like Karate, Kung-fu, and Taekwondo, and have nothing to do with Filipino martial arts proper. Practitioners of this art feel that patterning one's training and techniques after those arts of another country does much to confine the spontaneity and true nature of their indigenous fighting methods.

The many techniques of this art are trained, however, through a number and variety of solo and partner practices, wherein nothing is pre-set or limited, though looping programs are employed for a so called "thousand experience." Thus, if using the empty hands, one can employ the forearms, hooking, joint manipulation, braking, adhering, and so on either in the air against imaginary opponents or with a partner against any type of attack, and for as long as one feels necessary. The same holds true for weapons practice. Thus, spontaneous, free-flowing movements and improvised combinations are both the means and the ends, wherein there are neither set beginnings nor endings to movements, techniques, or one's training.

Fighting Strategies

Fighting strategies in Kalis Kalis ng Tinagalogan are more articulated than the drills used to train them. The first rule of engagement is to "disengage." Should one not be able to disengage their opponent, than they are to attack first (or attack later) when the enemy least expects it.

Other strategies include never going against the force of an attack, but flowing with the force of change by utilizing the ways of effortlessness, patience, and compassion.

Another key strategy is to know when to hold on and when to let go. This is steeped in the analogy of a boat and its inherent value. Value is like a boat, beliefs are like the rowing paddles, and compassion is like the water. If you are not on the water, don't row your boat as if you were. And after crossing the water, let go of your boat, your rowing paddles, and don't look back at the water, but move on with the flow, the force, and the way.

In application, this strategic philosophy encompasses such things as not putting yourself in a position where your opponent can do to you what you can do to him, as such is inferior positioning. And never start a fight you can't finish and with possible consequences you can't swallow.

Moreover, don't close all your windows where the thief might come in if you want to catch him, but open up one then close it, open up another then close it. When the intelligent thief sees your pattern, he'll anticipate your next opening. As you open your next window, you'd welcome him and there you'd catch him and cut off his hand.

Perhaps one of the most essential strategies or philosophies adhered to is to use the way of cause and effect to learn to suspend compassion and to not hesitate to utilize the enemy's evil flow of aggressive force to stop him.

Free-Sparring

Since practitioners of Kalis Kalis ng Tinagalogan believe their art to be "ancient," they do not believe in sparring. In the ancient times, when one challenged another to spar, it usually was a challenge of honor, and the sparring often ended with the death of one and the crippling of the other. Therefore, the word "competition" is a foreign concept to this art.

That Kalis Kalis ng Tinagalogan has been handed down in "the secret magic circle" for generations, exponents feel no need to "prove" themselves to practitioners of other arts through silly, rule-bound sparring competitions.

They know their art is effective through the orally transmitted exploits of past masters who fought valiantly in its name, some to have died in the process, utilizing their ways of *buno* ("killing").

Moreover, practitioners do not believe in "just going at it," wherein students can easily develop bad habits or limiting preconditioning. These are unproductive to one's training for reality, where they can gouge, bite, head butt, strike the back of the head, break the knees or elbows, choke, tear the esophagus, and so on all things forbidden in modern competitive sparring.

However, while sparring in itself is shunned, there is no substitute for experience. Therefore, this art utilizes basic free-flowing exercises where learning to read the constant flow of attack and a "thousand times" experiences of the same movement against a particular attack will be had as they flow with the changes of real (not pre-set) motion. Such training is all done in the safety of their training areas and under the guidance of Guro Omikl D.

Punong Guro Edgar G. Sulite

17

LAMECO ESKRIMA

Lameco Eskrima is a contemporary fighting art developed by the late Edgar G. Sulite. It is composed of eleven Filipino martial arts, of which the major systems are: De Campo Uno-Dos-Tres Orehenal (from Jose Caballero), Kalis Ilustrisimo (from Melicio and Antonio Ilustrisimo), Moderno Largos (from Jesus Abella), Pekiti Tirsia (from Conrado Tortal and Leo Gaje), and the Sulite family system (from Luis Sulite). As an underlying philosophy, the system embraces the "flow of nature," the "integration of mind, body, and spirit," and technique principles from the three main regions in the Philippines (Luzon, Visayas, and Mindanao).

Training Progressions

On the whole, Lameco Eskrima emphasizes training in the single stick *(solo baston)*, double sticks *(doble baston)*, sword and dagger *(espada y daga)*, single dagger *(solo daga)*, double daggers *(doble daga)*, single sword *(solo espada)*, and empty hands *(mano y mano)*.

Lameco Eskrima emphasizes the first five basic strikes *(cinco tero)* as the focal point of initial learning and development. Footwork is also learned and practiced as an integral part of this phase, after which the *abecedario* or twelve basic strikes of the system must be learned and mastered. The *abecedario* forms the basis for progressive instruction and identification of the different drills, patterns, and exercises that follow.

In tandem with these basic exercises, students progressively learn the *laban-laro* combat drills to develop their sense of coordination, distance, and timing. The *laban-laro* drills are practiced continuously with the partners switching offensive and defensive roles after each turn, and encompass series of offensive and defensive strikes, counters, and strategies.

A single training session usually covers all weapon categories, thus ensuring even growth and progress in the art. A student must show skill and understanding in his current level of instruction before proceeding to the next level. This does not mean, however, that they are denied exposure to further levels of training, but that they are made aware of the succeeding stages and the importance of the fundamental skills being developed in their current level. It is in this way that students are appreciative and cognizant of the importance of dedicated

training thorough an understanding of the required skills. This is a reflection of the art's motto: "Repetition is the mother of all skills."

Training Methods

In addition to repetitive training of footwork and strikes, Lameco Eskrima utilizes three solo single stick sets containing twelve drills each (thus becoming thirty-six drills) and thirty-six partner *laban-laro* pre-arranged fighting drills. These drills are staggered throughout the curriculum, and one set must be completed prior to moving on to the next. In addition, there are short forms for double sticks as well as the sword and dagger, but these are less defined and taught intermittently.

The extensive *laban-laro* drills develop the fluidity in technique that is necessary to effectively apply the art in the ever-shifting flow of combat. Practitioners continuously evolve from defensive movements to offensive movements while performing these drills without pause, just as would occur in actual combat.

Sulite is also credited with the development of the special hand protector as used in Lameco Eskrima, Kalis Ilustrisimo, and Bakbakan Kali. It is this training equipment that enables practitioners to engage in limited hand as well total body target striking, using padded or un-padded sticks. With the use of the hand protectors, practitioners are able to engage in *pata-maan,* or actual hitting, with limited chances of serious injury. This exercise greatly improves timing and distancing as well as developing compactness and battle-smart attributes.

What separates Lameco Eskrima from many of the contemporary Filipino systems is its emphasis on developing the totality of the human being through training mind, body, and

spirit, and not just the physical dimensions of the art. Attention, intention, visualization, and focus are considered integral components of this art and are a primary focus of the developmental training process.

Fighting Strategies

The term "Lameco" is derived from the first syllables of the three fighting ranges: *la* for *largo* or long range, *me* for *medio* or medium range, and *co* for *corto* or close range. The combat strategies employed in Lameco Eskrima are likewise applied in terms of these ranges.

Long range is that distance wherein the tips of the combatants' weapons can touch the extended weapon-holding hand. In this range, the weapon is unable to effectively hit the opponent, unless the opponent's arm is extended. Although most people have a tendency to fight defensively when in this combat range, it is also good for developing timing and footwork.

Medium range is that distance wherein the wrists of the two combatants can touch, and thus the weapon can hit the opponent's head. One must be extremely careful when in this range as it is much harder to block an opponent's strikes, as there are ample targets for the opponent to aim for. Footwork plays a paramount role in this combat range, as it serves as a transition for closing in or moving away from an opponent.

Close range is that distance wherein the combatants can touch shoulder to shoulder. It is different from the other ranges due to the closeness of the battle and diversity of available techniques. In essence, anything can happen.

True to its name, Lameco's fighting strategy insists on being able to fight effectively in each of the three combat ranges. This is in part dependent on effectively changing combat

ranges and spatial relationship relative to the opponent as a means of baiting him or putting him in a precarious position.

Thus, the patterns of footwork from various major systems are integrated into the techniques at each range. The signature forward and back shuffle of the Caballero system accompanied by its devastating "meteoric" strikes is but one of the now easily recognizable techniques of a Lameco fighter. Likewise, the *lutang,* or hanging footwork, accompanied by the compact and swift execution of the *bagsak,* or drop strike, of Kalis Ilustrisimo has become the hallmark of the seasoned Lameco practitioner. In addition to these primary movement strategies, Lameco's use of triangular and shifting footwork reflect its Filipino roots. It is the footwork, accompanied by the *enganyo* or feinting techniques, that makes the Lameco practitioner effective in combat.

Free-Sparring

Lameco Eskrima places heavy emphasis on sparring, as it is viewed as a method of acquiring unlimited combat experience. Moreover, only the zeal, courage, and dedication of the practitioner limit the amount of skill, experience, and knowledge that can be extracted from sparring.

Frequent sparring and application of techniques develop and actualize the art's strategies. Without free sparring, drills remain drills. They will be nothing more than mere exercises and movements that create the illusion of skill without the reality of combat.

It is only through constant and regular free-style sparring that the techniques become truly honed, reflexive movements. Without the active participation of the mind, body, and spirit under the stress of sparring or actual engagement, the techniques will remain mere physical exercises without any relationship to combat.

Sparring is done in stages to gradually orient the practitioner to the demands and reality of combat. Beginning with the basic but demanding hand target sparring, students proceed to padded stick sparring with minimum armor to develop awareness and respect for their weapon. And while many systems encourage weapon sparring while wearing full protective equipment, practitioners of Lameco Eskrima believe that this tends to completely ignore reality. Rather, practitioners are required to use minimal protective equipment to encourage the development of defensive skills and not just offensive techniques.

The final goal of sparring is to engage in matches with "live" (unpadded) sticks. By this stage, the Lameco practitioner is cognizant of the demands of combat and confident in his sparring skills. In the words of Sulite, "To develop self-confidence is to do the things you fear to do." And, "Always ponder to your experience, for it is the best teacher."

Grandmaster Filemon E. Caburnay

18

Lapunti Arnis de Abaniko

The art of Lapunti Arnis de Abaniko was co-founded by Filemon Caburnay and Johnny Chiuten, Jr, and is a synthesis of their respective training—Caburnay's Visayan Arnis and Chiuten's southern Shaolin Kung-fu. It also incorporates other techniques that both masters learned outside of their main systems, including: Arnis, Escrima, Shaolin, Aikido, Tai Chi, Karate, Pa-Kua, and Hsing-I. This vast expertise informs the different techniques of the art. As a term, Lapunti is an acronym of the three *barrios* on the island of Cebu where it originated: Labangon, Punta, and Tisa; Arnis is the art of stick fighting; and Abaniko is the fanning motions so prevalent in the system.

Training Progressions

The training curriculum of Lapunti Arnis de Abaniko maintains different categories, including: single stick *(solo baston)*, stick/sword and dagger *(espada y daga)*, double sticks *(doble baston)*, knife *(daga)*, and empty hands *(pangamot)*.

Beginners start with the basic stances, incorporating the scissors stance from Johnny Chiuten's Kung-fu style, and the basic twelve strike, three strike, five strike, and seven strike combinations of Arnis. Following the stances and strikes come sets of exercises with the hands or weapons, whose concepts are patterned after the pre-set *kata* of Karate and *hsing* of Kung-fu.

Following the solo forms, and interwoven within the curriculum, are attack and defense partner exercises. These train skills in *palakaw* (feints, entrapments), *tapi-tapi* (checking), and *trangkada* (locking), which are traditional in Arnis, both with different weapons and with the empty hands.

The goal of these drills is to prepare students for free-sparring. Sparring in Lapunti Arnis de Anabiko is done with the single stick, double sticks, long and short sticks, training knife, and the empty hands.

There is no absolute fixed period of time a student must spend in this art to progress to new material. Rather, it depends on the ability of the student and the amount of time spent on a technique or course of instruction. It is the instructor who determines if a student has made sufficient progress and is ready for the next stage.

However, to set this system in place and to develop in students a high level of skill takes time. There are really very few students who have the commitment, dedication, talent, and stamina to pursue that goal. The quest takes years. There are many stories of half-serious people who go from teacher to teacher. When viewed by exponents of Lapunti, they are like the ducks who float on the surface, never really going deep, even to feed. What teachers of this art prefer in their students are cormorants—birds that dive down and don't come up for air for long periods of time, until they catch their quarry.

Training Methods

There are a number of pre-arranged training forms utilized in Lapunti Arnis de Abaniko. They teach the different blocks and strikes from different postures and incorporate movement in different directions with and without weapons. These forms are required especially of

beginners who must develop their vocabulary of movement.

The forms are essential for training students in the following areas: basic stances, which incorporate the style's signature cross-legged stances for advancing, retreating, or changing directions; ground-fighting with or without weapons; the meditations *(orasyones)* for developing sensitivity to the five directions and others; the use of locking, holding, and releasing techniques; the study of the anatomical and energetic vulnerabilities of the human body.

Through proper training and study of the forms, practitioners are able to learn the strengths and weaknesses of the human body, both in its physical and energy manifestations.

Fighting Strategies

Lapunti co-founder Johnny Chiuten is responsible for developing and putting into effect the three principal fighting strategies of this style.

The primary strategy is known as "technique to technique." This strategy asserts that there are any number of techniques to counter any given technique an opponent might attack with. When an opponent has committed himself to a posture or movement, there are different ways to address it. Thus, students come to learn and embrace the different possibilities of combat that emerge at different times.

The second principal strategy is for the practitioner to break his rhythm and/or direction of movement. By doing this the practitioner can effectively create an anticipation on

the part of the opponent with his stick or body and then break from it. This strategy is commonly known as *enganyo* (feinting) but is more elaborate than the word suggests. It incorporates body weaving *(sawali)*, directional movements *(kumpas)*, and snake-like movements *(balitok)*.

The third principal strategy is for the practitioner to move in the direction the opponent least expects him to go. This requires an intricate understanding and application of the system's different stances. Lapunti has many postural shifts that are unpredictable, and thus effective.

There are other fighting strategies employed in Lapunti Arnis de Abaniko. As countless techniques have been integrated into the art's repertoire. These are incorporated into the training and rehearsed so that practitioners are able to develop the ability to apply them in actual combat. It is a gradual progression through slow exposure to different techniques.

Free-Sparring

Being able to effectively employ the art in free-sparring is the goal of Lapunti training. Free-sparring incorporates different distances and techniques for long, medium, and close combat ranges, outside and inside defenses and attacks.

Students progress from stage to stage until their techniques become intuitive. When they develop a large vocabulary of combat, they are permitted and encouraged to do light sparring and then move on to a more "free form" encounters. A good instructor should be able to see at what stage the student is in by his performance in sparring.

As Lapunti practitioners believe that the use of armor and protective equipment diminishes the reality of the fight, none is used during free-sparring sessions. It has been found that when worn, the participants become reckless, their movements become inhibited, their sense of distance becomes impaired. The sparring becomes what is called *bara-bara,* or wild striking movements. With extreme precision, practitioners must learn to distance themselves and focus their strikes— skills only developed through unarmored sparring. They must develop a serenity of mind and a certainty of purpose.

Safety in training is also a key to developing skill, thus some strikes and targets are prohibited when sparring, such as strikes aimed at the eyes or the head. If such potentially lethal strikes are used, they should be focused so that the stick stops short of impact.

Practitioners of Lapunti Arnis de Abaniko believe there is something elemental about fighting. It is a reenactment of a primal era when man had to fight for his survival. With nothing but himself between life and death, the drama became intense and fatal. Early humans therefore imitated animals to develop the weapons for the hunt. And humans had the brain and the cunning to develop strategy for combat.

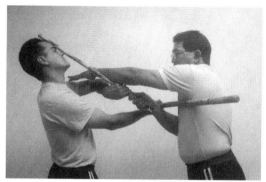

Armor detracts from that drama. Of course, minimal protection may be used by those who do not feel comfortable about being hit. Goggles, for instance, and helmets may be worn to cover the eyes and head. In the West, where there is a sense of litigiousness, instructors would rather that students signed a waiver and wore an armor. After all, getting sued is a big consideration in teaching these days.

Grandmaster René Latosa

19

LATOSA ESCRIMA

Latosa Escrima was developed by Rene Latosa, whose experience in Filipino martial arts spans more than thirty years. Beginning in 1968, Latosa studied Serrada Escrima under the late Angel Cabales and Dentoy Revillar, Kadena de Mano under Maximo Sarmiento, and Larga Mano under Leo Giron. His most influential teacher was his own father, Juan Latosa, who did not emphasize a specific name to his art, just that it was effective.

Training Progressions

As a system, Latosa Escrima has been called "Combat Escrima," as its techniques and concepts are steeped in reality-based encounters and applications. And while the system has a limited number of techniques, all of its basic training and drills are grounded in a core set of concepts and principles that can be effectively applied to any weapon, such as the staff, knife, sword, side-handle baton, stick, palm stick, spear, shield, and empty hands.

There are twenty-two levels of promotion in Latosa Escrima: twelve student levels, five technical levels, four master levels, and the title of grandmaster.

Regardless of rank, the basic philosophy to learning and then applying weapons is based on the concept of "transition." That is, the universal application of basic fighting concepts to all weapons and the empty hands. With this method, one need not learn different means of wielding and employing a staff than a knife, as their respective movements are steeped in the same basic conceptual framework of proper balance, power, timing, distance, speed, focus, and generalized movement angles. In other words: "Keep it simple to be effective."

The system employs basic training methods to help students understand the reasoning behind the techniques and the concepts of Escrima. The philosophy behind the Latosa Escrima system is very simple: "The whole is greater than the sum of its parts." For example, a technique cannot exploit its full potential unless combined with the attributes of balance, power, speed, focus, timing, and attitude. When combined, these elements cause the outcome or whole to be more effective then the sum of the parts. In this system, then, the number of different techniques mastered by an individual does not necessarily increase his level of competence. Thus, quantity of techniques and weapons learned is not the focus.

Nevertheless, techniques are tools used to understand, accept, and retain ideas, and so they are taught.

Techniques are practiced movements until combined with the proper fighting concepts. The progression from a beginner to an advanced student is to understand the concepts which underlie the techniques. Thus, one's true progression in this art is based on conceptual understanding and practical application of basic concepts and movements into meaningful techniques with various weapons. As an example, as a beginner a student learns about the elementary concepts of balance; as an intermediate student his grasp of balance should be better focused than the beginner; and when the student reaches advanced stages, the concept of balance should be refined.

This training method plays more to the self motivational arena, whereas if you reach the eleventh student level, your application should be more noticeable than one at the ninth level. Therefore, students earn their rank levels based on depth of technical knowledge, not on sheer number of techniques performed well.

As a rule based in necessity of time in understanding, practitioners must spend more time in the advanced student levels (eight through twelve) and on the five technical levels, than on the lower student levels. In general, however, student levels require a minimum time in grade of one to four

months each, while in the technical levels a year or more per level is required.

Training Methods

There are a number of training methods and drills utilized in Latosa Escrima. However, as with the stress on understanding concepts for rank promotion, many of the drills and training methods relate to individualizing concepts. In other words, they are concerned not as much with memorization of pre-determined techniques merely executed technically well, but with isolating the basic concepts so when the movement or combination is applied, the practitioner doesn't lose the concepts, overstep boundaries of efficacy, or open himself to potentially deadly counter blows.

The training methods, then, are looked to as mechanisms for improving techniques and concept application. When practicing a drill based on the "figure eight" striking motion, for example, practitioners take each hit of the figure eight and execute the basic concepts. They then consider the following: Does each hit have power and speed? Is the body balanced when executing the movement while actually striking an opponent or object? Does the striker create timing patterns his opponent can attune to? Where is the practitioner's body momentum when striking?

And while the figure-eight movement is found in virtually every Arnis and Escrima system and is easy to execute, few truly understand its inherent value. One must consider if this common strike is really a conglomerate of individual hits, a series of combinations, a series of timing and off-timing patterns—either offensive or defensive. Latosa Escrima tests its defensive components to see if they would

stop a person of similar expertise, of faster speed, of greater strength, of larger body size and weight, and so on.

Thus, while Latosa Escrima employs many of the generic drills and training methods found in other styles, what sets this art apart is its practitioners' deep understanding of the reality of all their basic movements and concepts. They believe training is a deeper process than merely understanding the movements of each technique.

Again, while solo forms are practiced in this system, they are not pre-arranged. After all, when one practices defined forms, restricted freedom of expression is often the result. And while forms may be a defining factor in a system, they are usually someone else's design and not that of the individual practitioner. The forms in Latosa Escrima, then, are created around defined concepts. Instructors want to see in their students while performing the form the application of power, speed, offensive movements, distance, timing, balance, off-lining, and other attributes. Furthermore, it matters not what types or combinations of offensive movements the students choreograph in their forms, as long as the concept format is utilized. Forms, then, exist in this art for the individual students to retain ideas and train fighting concepts.

Fighting Strategies

The fighting strategy of Latosa Escrima is to simply be prepared for combat and to never violate the concepts and principles inherent in the art's techniques and training scheme.

The bare bones of the system's techniques is known as "the box," which consists of five interrelated offensive movements. These movements may seem as if they fall into the definition of blocks, but they are actually interference strikes. The idea is to understand the movements of a technique and then to relate this to every concept studied in the art. With only five main movements in the system, the approach is simple, yet the variety endless.

Another key strategy is for practitioners to be realistic about their art and their own abilities to apply it. It is with this in mind that practitioners understand the various risks in thinking in "perfect world" terms, such as "hit me here and hit me perfectly and I will respond in such a way." Most martial arts training is done this way, and rightfully so because of certain liabilities. Thus, students come to realize that training is done

in a "stop time" mode conducive to learning. However, true understanding of the movements is a distinct and different reality. Through years of teaching, testing, and developing fighting concepts, Rene Latosa is a believer in "using what works" in real life situations. It is very important to feel positive and confident that the knowledge will prove to be an advantage when called upon to utilize it in combat. The system holds that having a great offense is, as in most contact sports, the best defense.

The main component to the Latosa Escrima fighting strategy is in the area called "pre-fight." This is the area when you begin to build your strategy around the environment (solid ground, wet land, gravel, near obstacles, other people around), the opponent (whether he is big, strong, tall, what weapon he has, who is with him, etc.), when you get ready (the position of your hands, giving away your strategy too early, the position of your body, whether you have a weapon or not), and finally whether you strike first (determined by analysis of risk, protection of life and property), and so on.

The idea of blocking comes at the second phase, when the practitioner's options have run out or they only have limited options left because they didn't apply the pre-fight strategy. The reality check comes when they see an opponent approaching with a weapon and wait until he strikes. If they wait this long to respond, they better pray their reaction speed is supersonic!

Free Sparring

There is no free-sparring *per se* found in Latosa Escrima. Daily reality training is steeped in a multitude of training drills where the hitting is constant and the distance between practitioners is maintained. Since these drills evolve into free-form or spontaneous striking training, they become known as "free drills."

And while practitioners of Latosa Escrima do not "practice" free-sparring, they do apply their art and put it to the test in full-contact tournaments. And while they participate in other people's tournaments, they prefer to compete in those sponsored by their art, which in addition to stick striking, also includes punching, kicking, and grappling. And while their tournaments are rule-bound, they are scored much like boxing matches, where light hits count less then full powered hits, and the overall performance of the fighter is taken into account. Again, a more reality-based approach to application.

Grandmaster Benjamin Luna Lema

20

LIGHTNING SCIENTIFIC ARNIS INTERNATIONAL

After studying Arnis under his father, Juan, in Mambusao, Capiz, and then from a German-Filipino named Weinstein, Benjamin Luna Lema went around challenging and learning from other *arnisadores*. In 1937, Lema founded Lightning Scientific Arnis International, which is both the name of the fighting art and its governing organization.

Training Progressions

As a classical Arnis system, Lightning Scientific Arnis International encompasses four categories of training: single stick *(solo baston)*, double sticks *(doble baston)*, the concurrent use of a stick and knife *(espada y daga)*, and the empty hands *(mano-mano)*. Empty hand training emphasizes unarmed defense against weapons in addition to training in striking (although this aspect is a somewhat recent addition to the art). The emphasis of the art is on the single stick and the stick and dagger.

Like many of the elder Arnis masters, Lema does not make use of an extended curriculum but teaches a core set of techniques which is required of all students to learn. In an effort to perpetuate the art, though, Lema's protégé, Elmer Ybañez, structured a training and testing schedule around the material based on a defined five-level training progression. Thus, while the material is basically the same, the teaching approach between Lema and Ybañez varies. Given space limitations, we will concern ourselves here with the system as taught by its founder, Benjamin Luna Lema.

Before embarking on the training students are taught proper courtesy as expressed in salutations with the single stick, the double sticks, the stick and dagger, and the empty hands. Following basic courtesy, students are trained in the art's basic stances and stepping patterns, of which there are two: *kambio* and *segida*. *Kambio,* which literally means "to shift," is a form of displacement, whereby the lead foot is placed at an angle to the rear foot. The practitioner may be in either a front stance or a horse stance, but at roughly a forty-five degree angle to the front. The rear foot advances to the front, at a point roughly a shoulder's width apart from the other foot, while the lead foot then steps back to the rear. The same angle is thus maintained, but with a different lead.

Segida, on the other hand, is a shuffle-step to the front or to the side.

The thirteen basic strikes of the system are taught next. The thirteen strikes are initially taught as target areas on an opponent. Once students memorize the proper location of strikes, they are taught how to execute them with speed, timing, precision, follow-through, and with proper mechanics of the waist and shoulders to generate power.

The thirteen strikes are followed by what is termed the "twelve methods." These are various combinations of strikes, progressing from the simple diagonal strikes of the first method, to the close-in block-and-counters of the second and third methods, to more complicated maneuvers. The "twelve methods" include ways of striking at reverse angles (like diagonal upward and diagonal downward), how to perform the figure-eight maneuvers, how to execute double strikes along the same angle *(doblada),* and so on.

Once proficiency in the "twelve methods" is achieved, students progress to *bigay-tama,* the first of the many two-person drills found within the system. Here the use of stepping patterns in conjunction with stick movements is taught. Half-striking from both open and closed angles are taught as means of counter-striking. Many of the movements taught in the "twelve methods" are also applied here. Again, proper body

mechanics are stressed throughout every movement.

When the student can display ease of movement in the *bigay-tama* and can recognize attacks approaching from different angles, the next stage of training is *espada y daga serrada*. This is a close-quarter stick and dagger training drill, wherein one must effectively block and counter his opponent's random attacks. The drill is first taught using the single stick to learn coordination, and progresses to *espada y daga*.

When the practitioner can flow from strike to strike within *espada y daga serrada,* disarming maneuvers are added to the drill. There are two modes of training disarms: stick against stick and empty hands against stick. The techniques are first taught in sequential order according to difficulty. Later on, practitioners are taught how to counter these techniques and then how to reverse the counters.

The above is the general training students receive in the system. For those who are able to persist, more advanced training beyond the core curriculum is available. Such advanced training includes *bigay-tama* using *espada y daga,* wherein both combative elements are combined. For the more advanced students, this drill is done using a real knife, as opposed to an aluminum or wooden training dagger, and both the stick and knife attacks are done at high speed, while maintaining an element of control for safety.

Other advanced training includes techniques of *espada y daga* versus *espada y daga* drilled in a semi-freestyle fashion. Then there are the many disarming defenses against the stick and the knife. This material is often demonstrated in public as a means of displaying the skills of the Lightning Scientific Arnis International practitioner. The final advanced stage encompasses the unarmed applications of the weapon movements, as translated into joint locks, throws, punches, and kicks.

Then there is also special material that is not generally shown to the public (which, of course, can not be divulged here). It should also be noted that Lema is often revising and updating his system, constantly looking for ways to improve it. Thus, it is a living, growing, adapting system whose curriculum is molded to fit the times.

Advancement through the material and stages of the system is based on several factors. If the testing schedule is followed, with an average of four to six months between each test, a student can test for all the material between two and two-and-a-half years, assuming he comes to class at least three times per week and practices on his own. In reality, though, much of the material is introduced earlier than the testing schedule. This is, of course, dependent on the proficiency of the student in question.

Other promotion factors include: control (the ability of the practitioner to handle his weapon such as not to cause unnecessary injury, but while still retaining the combative intent of the maneuver); flexibility (the ability of the practitioner to switch techniques within a given session); and, perhaps most important, flow (the ability of the practitioner to move with the techniques of the style, whether one is drilling against another practitioner or on one's own).

Training Methods

The training methods of Lightning Scientific Arnis International are basically a reflection of the system's curriculum: thirteen basic strikes, eleven blocks, the twelve methods, sixteen combination drills, *bigay-tama, espada y daga serrada* (using the free hand), *espada y daga* (using the dagger), *espada y daga bigay-tama* (combined drills and their variations), stick versus stick disarms, and empty hand disarming of the stick.

As an example of the structure and progression of a core drill, the *bigay-tama* is taught as follows: An opponent's strikes, and his stick is parried by the defender's stick, while the defender's empty hand traps the opponent's arm. Then the defender counters with a variety of movements against the attacker's arm, body, and head. The student is taught to work both the inside and outside angles. At first, the applications of the second, third, and twelfth methods are introduced here since they emphasize the close-in nature of *ser-rada.* The applications of the other methods using this format are included later.

The main emphasis of this training drill is to teach practitioners how to flow and move from strike to strike. In real combat, there may not be enough time to use that many strikes, but the value of the drill is in teaching practitioners how to feel their way through different angles of attack, how to travel along each one, and how to feel the way an opponent may shift and change an angle of attack. In addition, the student's anaerobic endurance is built up, as a high-speed drill can leave him dripping with sweat, exhausted, and panting.

While Lightning Scientific Arnis International does not utilize pre-arranged fighting forms *per se,* it does employ standing forms, known as "methods" and "combinations." The methods are series of single strikes, with between two and four movements each. The combinations teach how to deliver multiple strikes along a single plane or direction. Thus, there could be two diagonal strikes along the same angle followed by a single diagonal strike along the opposite angle. These are introduced early in the curriculum and actually introduce students to a vast repertoire of techniques.

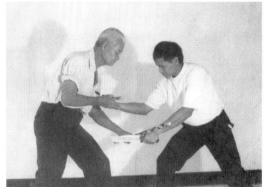

Fighting Strategies

Lightning Scientific Arnis International is first and foremost a fighting art, and second a sport. As such, it has seven clearly defined fighting strategies that must be understood by all students, practiced in drills, and applied in sparring.

The first strategy is to develop and always maintain proper technique form, as every movement must serve a purpose. The form of the techniques should reflect its combative use, especially since these are meant to be applied in combat. If it is not apparent that a movement can serve a direct and immediate use, it is discarded.

The second strategy is to "close the gate" from the outside. When fighting at intermediate to close ranges, the practitioner tries to close in on the opponent's attacking limb from the outside.

The third strategy is trapping, which is expressed together with the previous strategy of "closing the gate" from the outside. The traps flow out of the drills in *espada y daga serrada* and from *bigay-tama* and the combined drills stemming therefrom. Trapping is also expressed in the various disarming drills of the style. By trapping the opponent's attacking limbs, even momentarily, they are unable to strike you with them, or use them to block your own strikes.

The fourth strategy is to always follow-through every motion to its logical conclusion, as if the practitioner were striking through the opponent. Thus, if a strike meets a block, that block should bounce off the strike, and the strike should continue on to hit the opponent. This is where the power characteristic finds expression in combat.

The fifth strategy is to employ proper use of footwork together with the proper use of techniques. *Kambio* and *segida* help in the expression of proper form, closing the gate from the outside, trapping, and follow-through of all techniques.

The sixth strategy is that of maintaining and breaking rhythm. The partner drills teach rhythm and flow, but at the advanced level rhythm is set and then broken by the practitioners. This is usually initiated by the attacker in the drills.

The seventh strategy is to remember the stick is a stick. In contrast to Arnis systems that claim to use the stick as a metaphor for a bladed weapon, Lightning Scientific Arnis International emphasizes the use of the stick as a weapon in its own right. Thus, the applications and techniques reflect this orientation. It is possible to modify the movements of the system to reflect blade usage, but this is not widely practiced. It is a strategy of making use of your weapon's characteristics and potential to its fullest advantage.

Free-Sparring

Free-sparring is a mainstay of Lightning Scientific Arnis International, whose members follow the format developed by the National Arnis Association of the Philippines, which uses padded armor with headgear, face masks, gloves, arm guards, and elbow guards for protection.

Practitioners train for sparring by practicing their techniques on a hanging tire to develop power and follow-through skills, engage in running and rope skipping for endurance training, and practice the system's attack and defense drills using armor at full force. Then, of course, they spar.

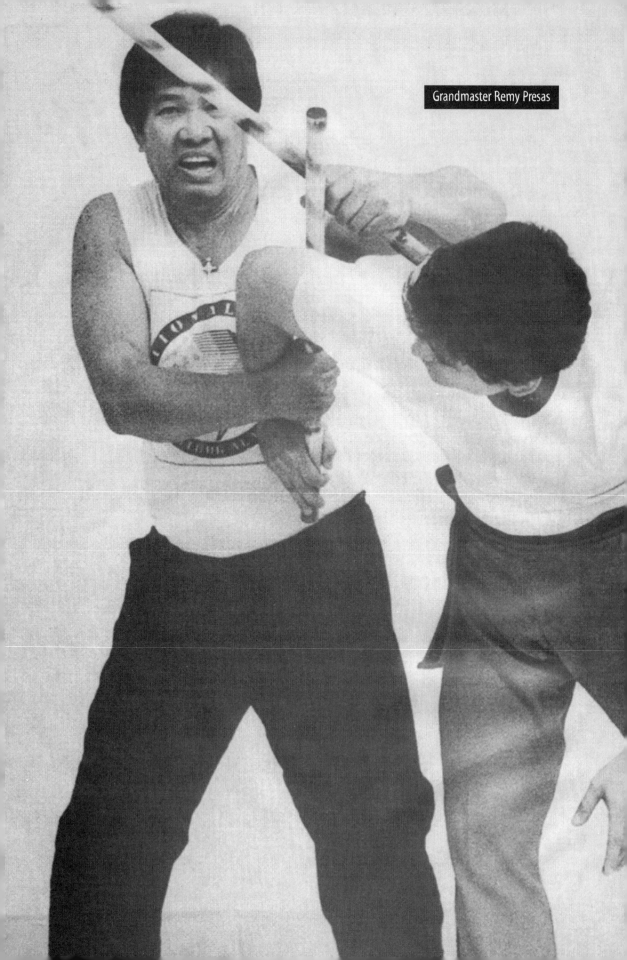

Grandmaster Remy Presas

21

MODERN ARNIS

In addition to studying the classical *espada y daga* style of his grandfather as a child, Remy Presas also studied the art of Balintawak Arnis. With a desire to bring Arnis into the mainstream Filipino consciousness, Presas devised a new system, based in simplicity, for the Philippine Department of Education. This new system he termed Modern Arnis, and it became standard curriculum in physical education classes in Manila. Presas later spread his art around the world while working for nine years as ambassador of goodwill for the Philippine Department of Tourism.

In the Philippines, Modern Arnis is also taught in the physical education and law enforcement settings by Remy's two brothers, Ernesto and Roberto—although they each have their own specialties. In the United States, it is Remy who is responsible for its spread and integration into hundreds of martial arts from other countries as their weapons training. It is no wonder Modern Arnis has become the most widely-practiced Filipino martial art in the world today.

Training Progressions

Although a contemporary system, Modern Arnis maintains the three classical training categories of single stick *(solo baston)*, double sticks *(doble baston)*, and stick and dagger *(espada y daga)*. One of the key developments making this art "modern" is the inclusion of a complete empty hand dimension (including strikes, kicks, sweeps, throws, traps, locks, disarms, and forms) that is lacking in the classical systems.

Along with the modern (post World War II) developments of Arnis in the Philippines, Modern Arnis has adopted a standardized and belt-denoted training scheme. The curriculum of the art is divided into eleven student ranking levels and ten instructor ranking levels. Each rank goes by a level number (e.g., level one), its Filipino name (e.g., *antas isa*), and a specific belt color (e.g., white belt).

Since Modern Arnis was developed as a system of physical education, emphasis is placed on proper warm-up and limbering exercises. Prior to the start of technique training, students go through a series of hand and wrist loosening exercises, followed by a full-body limbering routine of ten exercises, with and without a weapon.

Where instruction is concerned, students are first taught the proper method of holding the stick, and then how to stand and move in their stances. The four primary stances in Modern Arnis are the attention, straddle leg, forward, back, and oblique forward stances. The three postures are the front facing, half front, and side facing postures. From these stances and postures various methods of shifting the body through stepping, sliding, and turning is carried out. Body shifting is one of the key elements in the art, as proper body shifting and angling allow the practitioner to be just out of range of his opponent's strikes, while still affording him full power in his blows.

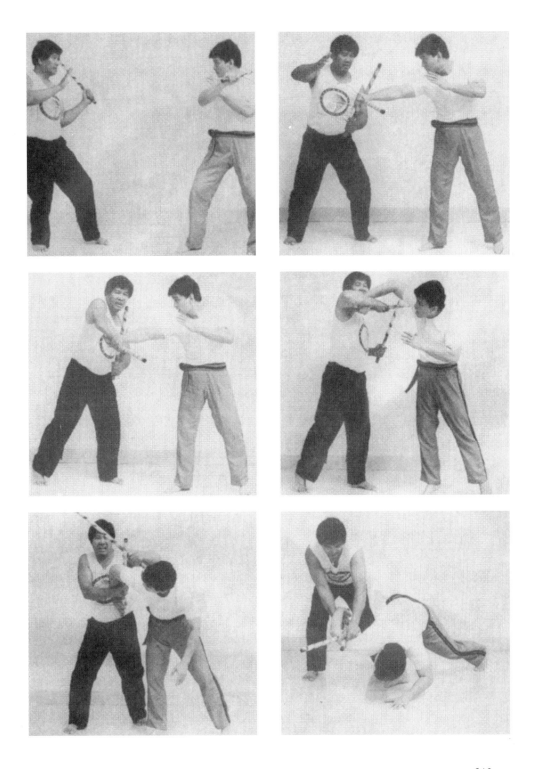

The system's twelve angles of attack are taught next, followed by their related defenses with the single stick. There are six primary blocking methods employed against specific angles, many of which may be used against a number of strikes. For example, the inward block is used against strikes two, four, seven, and eleven; the outward block is used against strikes one, three, six, and ten; the downward-inward block is used against strike 8; the downward-outward block is used against strike 9; the vertical block is used against strike five; and the rising block is used against strike twelve.

The basic defenses (whether armed or unarmed) are performed in a three-step process: 1) block the weapon, 2) grab the weapon, 3) counter attack. This method then advances to include trapping the attacking arm, off-balancing the opponent by pulling the attacking arm, or disarming the weapon and locking/throwing the opponent.

Following the single stick, students are introduced to the methods of *espada y daga,* or stick and dagger training. Stick and dagger training is based in the blocking techniques of X block *(equis),* cross block *(crossada),* umbrella block *(payong),* fan block *(abaniko),* stick and dagger parry *(palis-palis),* and the defensive countering "styles" (techniques) of double-zero strikes *(doblete),* side-to-side strikes *(banda y banda),* up-and-down strikes *(rompida),* and figure-eight strikes *(ocho-ocho).*

Stick and dagger training is followed by double sticks. The

double sticks are taught through the partner *sinawali* patterns. Pre-arranged sparring sets are introduced next, at which time practitioners learn to engage an opponent in a give-and-take manner. This is followed by disarming techniques, stick against stick and empty hands against stick techniques, and methods of empty hand trapping, striking, locking, and throwing.

Training Methods

The majority of training in Modern Arnis is done with a partner. Techniques are trained against an opponent executing single strikes in a give-and-take manner, wherein the attacker will execute the angle one strike, the other partner will block and counter. The first partner will then attack with an angle two strike, which the defender will block and counter, and so on.

Another training method is known as *de cadena*, or simply "the flow," and has empty hand and weapon variations. When unarmed, two partners engage in an equal exchange of attacks and defenses. In essence, one partner will strike, the other will parry and check the strike and then counter strike, with the first partner then parrying and checking and counter striking, and so on.

When the "flow" is performed with a weapon, either both partners can be armed with any weapon or just the attacker. In this drill variation, the attacker will strike along any angle of attack he wishes, but one at a time. The defender, weather armed or unarmed, will employ the *crossada* (crossing) style defense to simultaneously parry and strike/slice the opponent's attacking arm as each strike comes at him.

The *de cadena* flow drills are a principal method employed in Modern Arnis to develop in its practitioners the ability to react to an attack, respond accordingly, and be able to counter the attacker's possible counter, and to continue on without hesitation. Reflexes, timing, and distancing are the key attributes developed with this training.

A method employed to train ambidexterity, left/right coordination, and spatial relationship is *sinawali*. Single *sinawali* is first, which finds two people facing off and meeting each other's high and low strikes, first with the right hand and then with the left, repeating indefinitely. After a modicum of skill is gained using each hand separately, they are interwoven into sets of three strikes on each side. The basic three *sinawali* double stick patterns of all high strikes, combined high and low strikes, and all low strikes are used in Modern Arnis.

Another two-stick coordination drill is known as *redonda*, which is basically the linking of the all high *sinawali* pattern in a circular fashion. Power and precision in *redonda* is trained by having one partner holding two sticks extended at his side, which the other partner strikes three times to the right stick and three strikes to the left stick, and again. *Redonda* is also performed with all upward strikes, and this is known as "reverse *sinawali*."

The primary drill used to develop power, focus, and spatial relationship is known as "pre-arranged freestyle sparring," which is done in two stages. The first stage of the drill finds two practitioners engaging in a repetitive sequence of four strikes—forehand high, backhand low, backhand high, forehand low—and meeting each other's strike with the same strike. In other words, both partners strike at each other with the same sequence, their sticks meeting each other's in the middle.

The second stage of the drill finds the partners exchanging backhand strikes with the stick's butt-end *(punyo)*, using the left hand to parry the strikes.

The name of the drill itself is an oxymoron, as how can something be freestyle that is pre-arranged? However, there is a modicum of freestyle play in the drill, as partners can move between the two stages, going from a stick strike to a butt-end strike and back out again at random.

Aside from practicing the individual sequences in the air by oneself, the only other solo practice found in Modern Arnis are the solo forms, of which there are both armed and unarmed. As Presas is a former Japan Karate Federation member, his empty-hand forms were modeled after the *hein kata* of Shotokan Karate, and are merely Modern Arnis' representation of their movements and sequences. In other words, instead of a Karate block and punch, the forms use Arnis parries and strikes.

Fighting Strategies

There are two primary fighting strategies found in Modern Arnis proper. I say "proper," as the art has been incorporated into so many other systems that techniques, methods, and strategies of other arts have found their way into the curriculum of many of the art's instructors in the West.

The principal strategy is to employ the three-step defensive method. That is, block the on-coming strike to avoid injury, then use your secondary hand (or weapon) to immobilize the attacking limb (or weapon) so that it is temporarily out of the equation, and to then counter with a strike or locking technique to finish the altercation. This three-step process has a built-in safety factor and if performed properly can keep the opponent from initiating further attacks.

If the Modern Arnis practitioner is confronted with a seasoned fighter or improperly executes the block-trap-strike sequence, then he must employ the art's secondary strategy. As with its drills, this strategy is known as *de cadena* or "the flow." The strategy being to use the three-step defensive method to immobilize or otherwise entangle an opponent's limbs in such a way that he cannot maneuver properly. The flow also enables the practitioner the ability to react to, defend against, and counter a fast, skilled, or unpredictable opponent.

Free-Sparring

Keeping in mind that although Modern Arnis comes out of two classical systems, it was primarily developed as a method of physical education and secondarily as a self-defense system. As such, its sparring drill is pre-arranged to keep the chances of injury to a minimum, while still allowing practi-

tioners (e.g., high school students) to get a workout and gain some sparring skills.

However, as Modern Arnis spread around the world over the past thirty years, and many practitioners and teachers of the art come from different backgrounds, actual free-sparring has come into the curriculum to allow practitioners to compete on the tournament circuit. Sparring in this case is carried out while wearing full body armor and following the rules of the tournament setting.

Grandmaster Alejandro Abrian

22

MORO-MORO ORABES HENERAL

Alejandro "Andy" Abrian, the founder of Moro-Moro Orabes Heneral, was born on Samar island, Philippines, in 1937. He claims Arnis techniques came to him at the age of seventeen when he started striking two sticks hung from a rope at head and waist levels. That the *orabes* strike was his favorite, and that he later studied Boholano Arnis under a wandering master, Western boxing, and the dances of the *moro-moro* stage plays, Abrian named his art Moro-Moro Orabes Heneral.

Training Progressions

Although Moro-Moro Orabes Heneral does include training in stick and dagger and double sticks at its advanced levels, for practical self-defense purposes the art's focus is on single stick, single knife, and empty hand training.

Regarding the single stick, there are three categories of striking—twelve strikes, five strikes, and seven strikes—each with its own reasoning and purpose. The twelve striking sequence is taught first along with each strike's defensive blocking and countering techniques. Thus, from the outset students are taught to block, counter strike, and lock the opponent's attacking arm right away. And since there is no way to determine how an opponent will attack, and with which foot forward, Moro Moro Orabes Heneral does not train students in pre-set counters to specific attacks. Automatic movement and counters using the art's dynamic footwork and body shifting is the essence.

When swinging the stick, practitioners use their empty hand (left, if you are right handed) to propel the wrist of the weapon-holding arm to help generate power and speed. Moreover, while striking the foot moves with the strike at the same time. Shuffling backward, forward, and sideways in low stances is the norm.

Regarding the empty hands, the art seeks and employs nerve strikes and pressure point manipulation while holding, disarming, and throwing an opponent. Joint locking is a mainstay of the style, as are disarming techniques. And of course it is difficult to disarm without first locking if not immobilizing the attacking limb. There are roughly fifty basic disarms found in the curriculum.

Training Methods

As a fighting art steeped in practical techniques and training, Moro-Moro Orabes Heneral does not include a large number of training drills. Rather, fighting attributes are developed as fighting skills are learned and practiced. The key is to develop

the ability to effectively block, redirect, or avoid an opponent's strike and to then counter with speed and precision.

Of primary importance to effecting the art's techniques is fast and dynamic footwork. Indeed, among the various styles of Arnis and Escrima, the footwork of Moro-Moro Orabes Heneral is quite different. Footwork, and the techniques themselves, are done from a low, crouching position, wherein quick steps and shuffling maneuvers to the side and back of an opponent are performed while slipping under his attacks. Footwork is trained by itself in a dance-like fashion, with the practitioner moving in any number of directions to avoid imaginary attacks and to develop agility and stamina.

After the basic strikes and counters are mastered they are practiced conjointly with the footwork. In training application of the techniques, students merely perform them over and over again against an attacking opponent. Visualization plays a key role here, as students must develop the skills to not only block and counter a single strike, but to intuit where the opponent may strike next and place themselves in a safe position.

While there are no pre-set drills *per se* in this art, when its

techniques are linked together and performed in succession, they become drill-like. For example, one practitioner will strike another at random, who in turn must execute the proper defense and then counter the follow-up random strike or strikes. It is through this method that practitioners develop timing, rhythm, speed, and the ability to maneuver to the opponent's back or blind sides, thus hindering the execution of multiple striking combinations.

From this basic block and counter training, students progress to block and block and counter and counter training, wherein both partners block and counter at random in simulation of an actual (spontaneous) encounter. This training, again not in pre-set format but more like a drill, develops in practitioners honed reflexes, speed, maneuvering abilities, and spontaneous movement reactions. It is believed that this is the only way to truly develop realistic fighting skills, as pre-arranged drills are too limiting and students tend to get lost in them and focus on them with little regard for their purpose: fighting skills development and not skill in drill development.

As there are no pre-set partner training drills in Moro-Moro Orabes Heneral, there are no pre-set solo empty hand or weapon forms either. What is practiced, rather, are spontaneous, free-form attack and defense movements with either the single stick, single knife, or empty hands, wherein visualization plays a vital role. The creativity of the mind to counter existing techniques and to develop new counters or permutations of existing counters comes into play here, as the practitioner must visualize in his mind's eye the attacks of an opponent (or multiple opponents) and to then maneuver and counter effectively. The more creative the mind to direct the visualized opponent to attack and counter in fast and unpredictable ways, the better honed and agile skills the practitioner will develop.

Fighting Strategies

The primary fighting strategy in Moro-Moro Orabes Heneral is to pre-empt an opponent's movements, strike first, and strike hard. And if you can't strike first, then counter right away, be it with a stick, knife, empty hand strike, or joint lock.

When facing an opponent, practitioners hold their stick with the tip pointing down. This way, they believe, there is no opening in their guard. The fighting strategy here is to show your position to your opponent, wait for his strike, and then maneuver to his weak side and strike his newly-opened targets. Thus, giving the opponent the first move in which he will give up his guarded position and offer an opening through which the fight can be ended.

And while many Arnis systems employ striking sequences known as "angles of attack," practitioners generally strike without purpose. In contrast, the strategy employed when striking

or counter-striking in this system is to hit a target with a specific purpose in mind. As examples: strike the eyes so the opponent cannot see you; strike his arm so that he will either drop his weapon or be unable to move his arms with ease; and strike his feet so he cannot effectively utilize footwork.

If the opponent is skilled and the altercation cannot be ended quickly, then another key strategy is to remain calm and learn from the opponent while fighting. In other words, observe the openings the opponent offers when he strikes or maneuvers a certain way, remember them, and capitalize on them in the next available instance. And since most fighters tend to make use of the same strikes or combinations in a fight, the opportunity to observe the openings and exploit them one or more times to end the combative encounter will undoubtedly present itself.

Free-Sparring

Free-sparring as a sport is looked down upon by practitioners of Moro-Moro Orabes Heneral. Like pre-set drills and forms, practitioners view sport-like free-sparring as a possible trap students can get caught in. Often times, people get so caught up in succeeding in safe, rule-bound sparring sessions and competitions that they lose sight of the intended combative applications of their techniques. Rather than developing the skills to take-out an opponent quickly and effectively, they develop unnecessary multiple striking combinations to non-lethal, point-awarded targets, and the stamina necessary to keep up that pace of striking for minutes at a time. Real fights, especially those with weapons, don't last that long.

With this in mind, practitioners of Moro Moro Orabes

Heneral do fight one another, in addition to those willing practitioners of other styles. However, they do so sparingly and without the use of body armor or padded weapons. After all, rattan in itself is a lighter and more forgiving weapon than the hardwood sticks the art is supposed to employ, so to use padded rattan is viewed as ridiculous.

Before being permitted to spar, which is all-out, anything goes, students must first have spent five years in basic training of techniques and principles, and show mastery thereof.

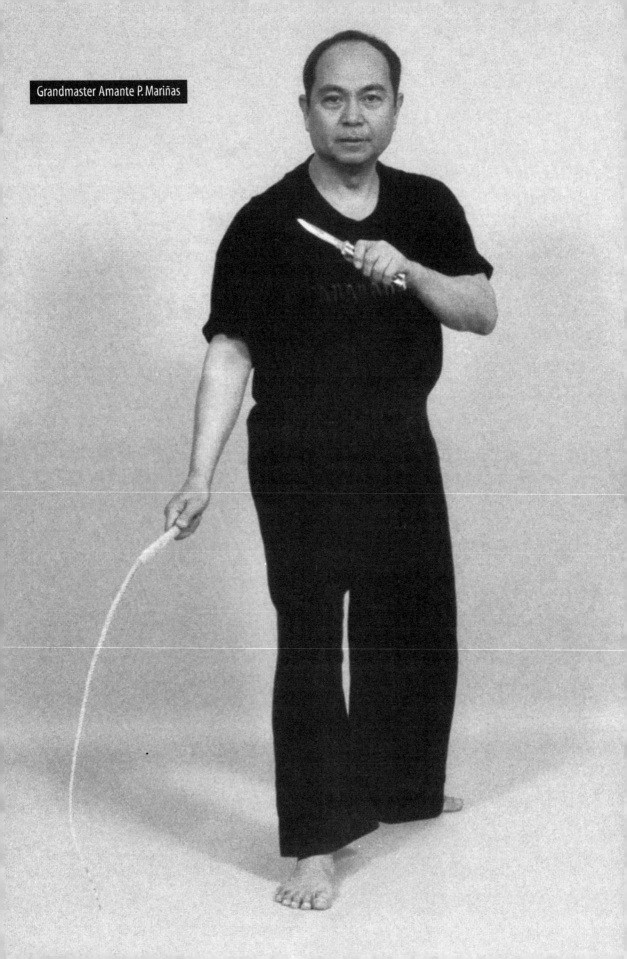

Grandmaster Amante P. Mariñas

23

PANANANDATA MARIÑAS

Pananandata is a Tagalog word for "the art of weaponry" in general as popularly used in the central Luzon region of the Philippines. The system of Pananandata Marinas is the specific weapon art founded by Amante Mariñas of Nueva Escija, and developed by him in the United States.

As a system, Pananandata Mariñas is solely concerned with the mastery of weapons—any and all weapons. Unlike many Filipino arts whose focus in on single stick, double sticks, and stick and dagger, this art also utilizes to great extent the horse whip, staff, throwing knives, side-handle baton, and a wide variety of other weapons.

Training Progressions

Training in Pananandata Mariñas is structured around the use of three broad classifications of weapons: 1) rigid weapons such as the stick *(yantok)*, staff *(pingga)*, and knife *(daga)*; 2) part rigid and part flexible weapons such as the dragon tail and the flail *(tabak toyok)*; and 3) flexible weapons such as the rope *(lubid)*, chain *(tanikala)*, butterfly knife *(balisong)*, throwing darts and knives *(bagakay)*, and blowgun *(zarhatan)*. In addition, empty hand fighting techniques are considered a natural outgrowth of training with weapons.

New students are first introduced to the methods of the single stick. After six months of practice they are introduced to the double sticks and distance or long-range sparring with one stick.

From the first year on, there are no sharp boundaries between training in one weapon and training in another, as it is based on the individual student's preference. As a general guideline, though, students may opt to learn the whip and rope after the first year of training; the *balisong* between the first and second year; the staff after the second year; and the stick and dagger at around the third year of training.

Regardless of weapon(s) learned, free-sparring is emphasized, as opposed to basic training and drills. In fact, after two years of study, students are required to free-spar in round-robin fashion without the use of body armor.

There is also no fixed time a student must spend on any given weapon before beginning another; it depends on the student's ability and desire. There is one guideline, though, which is that students are urged to work on those weapons they like the least, so as to make their weakness their strength.

At the end of the fifth year of training, practitioners of Pananandata Mariñas are required to concentrate their efforts on the particular weapon(s) of their choice. In this manner, they are able to master at least one weapon, and to then be promoted to instructor of that weapon within the system. Testing for instructor is only offered to deserving students who have been training regularly for at least seven years.

With this method of promotion, practitioners can become instructors in their area of specialty, without being held to

master all ten of the art's basic weapons. However, as they are recognized as instructors or masters of, say, the single stick or rope arts of Pananandata Mariñas, they are not necessarily considered instructors or masters of the system as a whole. Those who wish to be instructors of the art proper must spend considerable time mastering each weapon, one by one.

Training Methods

Repetition in training is a key component of Pananandata Mariñas. If fact, aside from emphasis on sparring, countless hours are spent in repetition of the basic movements of the system and of each specific weapon.

Regarding footwork, there are thirty sets of foot exercises for knife fighting and fifty sets for stick fighting. While there are overlaps within the sets, when linked one after another, it takes more than one hour to complete the entire series. Hence, they not only develop agility, mobility, and endurance, but are looked to as warm-up exercises to be done at the onset of training sessions. The art's footwork is based on that of two great Western champions whose success was grounded in their dynamic mobility: the boxing champion Muhammad Ali and the fencing master Aldo Nadi.

The are twenty-two basic striking techniques employed with the *yantok* (single stick), not including sweeping and twirling motions. Again, repetition is the key, and in any given training session students are found executing at least 2,500 strikes and thrusts. However, it is held that for students to improve at a reasonable rate, they must execute no less than 5,000 properly-executed strikes and thrusts per day.

While this may seem excessive, Mariñas thinks not and his striking precision and endurance is a testament to this training.

In fact, in his heyday, Mariñas himself used to perform 10,000 strikes per day—although this has tapered off to 2,000 daily in recent years to allow for repetitious training in other areas.

Another area of specified training is in the development and use of the left (or non-dominant) hand. Ambidexterity is achieved by training in both the double sticks and the *balisong*. In fact, advanced students are required to do the opening of the *balisong* in the left hand while concurrently wielding either a *yantok, latiko, hawakan, tabak toyok,* or another *balisong* in their right hand. Thus, they develop not only ambidexterity but the ability to use paired weapons of similar or differing functional values.

The empty hands are trained in eighteen sets of techniques.

These sets can be performed in a series, one at a time, or in sets of a specified number.

Pananandata Mariñas also employs training forms or striking combinations. There are fifty-two such forms, which can be performed solo or in pairs. While the combinations are important for coordination and technique templates, students are encouraged not to memorize them, but extract their essence, using them merely as striking templates.

In essence, though, the forms contain a basic four-fold structure: 1) They are short, running between four and ten movements each; 2) Deception is built into the movement sequences; 3) They incorporate abrupt changes in direction as well as the smooth flow of one technique into the next; 4) Each movement reinforces the next. Momentum builds up until the final hit where the greatest power is delivered.

There is no set time requirement to progress through the system or learning its forms. As a general rule, forms are taught after a student has gained solid experience in free-sparring. Having used this method for many years—which seems in contrast to training in most arts—students find marked improvements in their free-sparring skills.

Fighting Strategies

Practitioners of Pananandata Mariñas summarize their core fighting strategy by quoting a description of a Philippine dance made by a Spanish historian and translated by E. Blair and J. Robertson. The dance was thus described: "The dancers performed movements that were now slow, now rapid; now they attack, now they retire; now they come close, now they go away; now they incite, now they pacify..."

"Now slow, now rapid" indicates hand or foot speed; "Now

they attack, now they retire" indicates hand and foot movements, as any attack can provoke a reaction from the opponent which will reveal the patterns of his responses. Yielding ground must be part of any strategy, and not a matter of habit. "Now they come close, now they go away" indicates instinctive distancing, which will confuse the opponent's sense of distance. "Now they incite, now they pacify" regards forcing unnecessary angered emotions in the opponent to force a premature response to ensure a better chance of victory. After all, wild emotions often lose an otherwise winnable fight.

Another strategy employed is that of confusing an opponent as to the speed, power, direction, and timing of an attack. False attacks, feints, changes in tempo, and changes in distance all help to confuse the opponent. These could provoke the opponent into reacting the wrong way, thus creating an opening. However, one can only take advantage of an opening if they have trained hard, and correctly.

Free-Sparring

As evidenced throughout, unarmored free-sparring is the main focus and purpose of this fighting art. In each training session, practitioners are required to participate in twenty, twenty-five-second rounds of distance sparring—that is, where a fixed distance is set between opponents. They are not allowed to move their feet. The distance kept is such that one or the other partner can only reach the middle of his partner's stick. No body contact is allowed.

Distance sparring is a good way to introduce beginners to free-sparring without the initial fear of being injured. In addition, with this method of sparring the novice is only allowed to defend, thus developing defensive skills, patience, proper timing, and economy of movement.

Advanced students are required to engage in round-robin style free-sparring, from all distances and with all techniques. Again, no armor is worn, which trains emotional control as when students get hit they are not permitted to show it. Round-robin sparring sessions are done every two weeks, unless an injury is sustained, in which case bruised students are permitted to rest for one month. By rest is meant no round-robin sparring, although they are still required to participate in distance sparring.

Pananandata Mariñas is concerned with developing in its practitioners the ability to fight effectively with many types of weapons. As such, free-sparring sessions are done with single and double sticks, concurrent use of a long and a short stick, with staff, horse whip, and wooden dagger. Philosophically, students are taught that free-sparring is not only a contest between combatants, but a process through which they come to know themselves.

Grandmaster Filemon Cañete

24

SAN MIGUEL ESKRIMA

San Miguel Eskrima was founded by the late Filemon "Momoy" de la Cuesta Cañete, and is considered the "old style" of the Doce Pares Association of Cebu. The name San Miguel both refers to St. Michael, the patron saint of Cebu, and to the unique cross-leg stance employed in the style. The name is rather contemporary and was coined to differentiate the classical style of Filemon Cañete from the more modern Doce Pares styles in existence today. Filemon Cañete credits Lorenzo and Teodoro Saavedra as his main influences.

Training Progressions

As a comprehensive fighting art, San Miguel Eskrima contains the following ten weapon categories: single stick *(garote)*, stick and dagger *(espada y daga)*, double sticks *(dos armas)*, whip *(latigo)*, chain *(cadena)*, throwing knife *(daga)*, spear *(sibat)*, fifty-inch long stick *(bangkaw)*, and Combat Judo (empty hands against knife). These categories are taught in a comprehensive four-level training curriculum.

Beginners are first taught the system's basic strikes with the single stick while standing stationary and then using body shifting to develop the concept of generating power from the legs and transferring it through the waist and out to the arm and weapon. This weight shifting in coordination with striking is the beginning of changes in footwork and positioning, and begins to teach students how to generate whole-body power. Diagonal and horizontal cuts are emphasized first, and later simple thrusts *(tusuk)*, arcing thrusts *(songkiti)*, and circular strikes *(redondo)*. The stationary striking exercises are called *amara*.

The dagger is introduced with the *uno-dos* movement, which is the basic of sword and dagger practice. At this point, forward and backward footwork is introduced and students begin to formally learn the San Miguel pre-arranged fighting form, the linchpin of practice.

While learning the San Miguel form, the system's twelve angles of attack are taught, as are the basic stick and dagger counters against them. In addition, basic parries and strikes with a partner in simple exercises with the *dos armas* (double sticks), *garote* (single stick), *pinute* (sword), and *bangkaw* (long stick) are taught to develop footwork, courage, and a sense of timing and engagement distance. Basic knife defenses are also taught at the basic level.

The second level focuses on counter and re-counter movements and techniques. Of central importance are the *media* to *corto* (medium to close) range drills, focusing on lines of engagement from the moment there is stick-to-stick contact. Techniques of locking, throwing, controlling, and disarming with sword and dagger are also taught at this time. They build from simple "strips" (disarms) of the opponent's weapons to more complex techniques which take into account possible responses to the initial disarm attempt. Other exercises such as *tres-tres* (three-three) and "zig-zag" drills are also taught here, as are the spear and its two-person exercises, other solo forms with the sword and dagger, and double stick striking patterns.

Level three represents a process of integration, wherein acquired basic skills are interwoven and connected to the whole of the system's structure. This integration is accomplished through practice of the *balle-balle redondo* and the *palusot* two-person exercises. At this point other weapons and training may be added freely as appropriate, such as the bullwhip, chain, throwing knife, and advanced solo forms. The San Miguel form and other forms are now performed with double sticks. Unarmed defenses against stick and knife are performed at higher speed and counter and re-counter concepts are added to their practice.

This progression to training takes anywhere from between nine months to one year to complete per level. The last level of integrating all of the exercises for free-style practice takes the longest amount of time and practice, and beyond that there is always room for improvement.

Training Methods

It can be said that every movement, even basic striking techniques, are considered training methods in San Miguel Eskrima. The basic weight shifting in coordination with striking at level one is the beginning of changes in footwork and positioning, and begins to teach practitioners how to generate whole-body power.

The San Miguel pre-arranged fighting form is the core of the system, as it holds within its structure all the necessary techniques and combinations. Practitioners perform its basic movements while incorporating retreating, advancing, and sidestepping footwork. The exercise consists of several hundred strikes and takes from eight to ten minutes to perform. In this way students internalize the basic *espada y daga* movements while conditioning the body and mind by developing endurance and concentration.

The style also makes use of basic parries and strikes with a partner in simple exercises with the double sticks, single stick, sword, and long stick to develop footwork, courage, and a sense of timing and engagement distance.

There are also a number of long, medium, and close range drills focusing on developing body shifting and positioning while countering and re-countering an opponent's movements. Each exercise addresses different possibilities that can occur at its specific range.

Other exercises such as *tres-tres* (three-three) drills employ blocks and counters with lateral movement, while the so-called "zig-zag" drills teach how to out-position an opponent using lateral movement.

In addition to the basic training exercises and two-person fighting exercises, San Miguel Eskrima also incorporates a number of integration drills, such as *balle-balle redondo*, which incorporates long and medium range techniques with con-

cepts of counter and re-counter while circling around an opponent. The drill is initially performed as a set sequence that is later performed in a more free-style manner as the student's skill increases. Another integration drill is *palusot,* which is a free-style close quarter sword and dagger exercise taught first without the dagger thrust for safety, and in order to develop the use of the dagger in controlling the opponents stick. As skill increases the drill is performed with the dagger thrust, thus allowing the full range of *espada y daga* techniques to unfold in an un-rehearsed manner.

In essence, San Miguel Eskrima is primarily an *espada y daga* or sword and dagger fighting art. The other weapon categories are included to round out the practitioner's skills. It is the opinion of some that Filemon Cañete was trying in his own way to develop a method of internalizing *espada y daga* movements and principles of distancing and timing that could be applied in a multitude of ways. The auxiliary weapons training, then, is in part designed to aid in this process of internalization.

Double stick training, for example, develops fluidity of movement, ambidexterity, and continuos striking. The spear, by the nature of its concurrent use of two hands on a single bar, helps the body coordinate and link its bilateral movements to develop integrated power. The long stick or staff also links the

two hands but in a different way, in addition to assisting with power development, and blocking or deflecting its powerful strokes teaches courage. The chain emphasizes wrist action, while the bullwhip develops principles of timing and whole body power in striking. The throwing knife, besides its obvious function, develops focus and concentration.

Fighting Strategies

Articulated fighting strategies in San Miguel Eskrima are few, but nonetheless essential. One strategy practitioners employ often is to change ranges and use evasive footwork to deliver powerful strikes to the hands followed by immediately moving in with the dagger to deliver a finishing thrust. When there is stick-to-stick contact, the dagger hand attacks the open line immediately or checks the opponent's stick to open a line of attack.

In the close range the dagger is used to hook, trap, control, and attack in order to keep pressure on the opponent and not allow him to mount a counterattack.

Footwork, body shifting, and precise understanding of the range of the dagger thrust is used to gain position and draw the opponent into an over-committed attack. One favorite strategy is to move outside the thrust to attack the open left side between the ribs.

Free-Sparring

Free-sparring is practiced in San Miguel Eskrima with the stick and dagger while wearing protective gear. It is optional for practitioners who desire to take their skills to that level. However, Momoy Cañete did not favor the use of protective gear when sparring. Protective gear is only useful if both participants understand that receiving a thrust means you have lost. All to often protective equipment allows the trading of blows, which is absurd when both participants are thrusting with daggers.

Therefore, practitioners of this art hold that it is more useful to engage in sparring when the drills have been mastered

and both participants have an understanding of the consequences of certain blows. Sparring with blades can only be done by skilled practitioners who have worked together for some time and have fine-tuned control over their movements and emotions.

Free-sparring is considered the least important exercise in the system. It is a test of technique and is to be used occasionally to see if the student understands the drills and forms and how they may be applied in an unrehearsed situation.

Master Jorge Lastra

25

SAYAS-LASTRA ARNIS

Sayas-Lastra Arnis is primarily a *largo mano* or long range blade fighting art whose roots come from Dalmacio O. Sayas. Sayas employed his fighting art during the Philippine Revolution and the Philippine Insurrection at the turn of the last century, where he survived nearly ten years of field combat. Dalmacio Sayas passed his art on to Jorge Lastra, who further developed his own style and interpretation of weapon and unarmed fighting.

In the late 1970s, Jorge founded the Sayas-Lastra Brotherhood of Arnis and taught the art on the United States' East Coast up to his death in 1986. Eddie Lastra, along with younger brother, Robert, and Jorge's son, Dennis, founded the Lastra School of Arnis in 1993 to carry on the teaching of their family art. The Sayas-Lastra system of Arnis is currently headed by Eddie Lastra, the maternal grandson of Dalmacio Sayas.

Training Progressions

Training categories in Sayas-Lastra Arnis include single stick *(solo baston)* and sword *(solo espada)*, double sticks *(doble baston)*, stick and dagger *(baston y daga)*, sword and dagger *(espada y daga)*, knife *(daga)*, short staff *(pingga)*, long staff *(tungkod)*, and the empty hands *(mano y mano)*.

Skills development in each category is divided in phases, of which there are five. The criterion that determines skill is the smoothness and spontaneity of applying knowledge. As such, a student is not graded on the quantity of techniques that they may know, but on the quality and depth of understanding of those techniques. Indeed, practitioners hold that it is better to know how to use one technique in a hundred situations than to know a hundred techniques for one situation.

While it is understood that students progress at different rates depending on their backgrounds and natural abilities, there is a general guideline as far as how soon students are introduced to the various categories of training within this system. Thus, regardless of skill, the first year of training in Sayas-Lastra Arnis is spent studying basic concepts, the use of single and double edged and impact weapons, and related empty hand and knife defensive concepts. Classical *espada y daga* training is introduced in the second year, and classical *largo mano* tactics in the third year. The fourth and fifth years focus on developing skills in knife fighting and in the use and application of the staff.

Training Methods

Footwork and mobility is the key to effecting the long range techniques of this art. Footwork is based on double triangles known as "hourglass" and "diamond" patterns. These patterns naturally developed as a result of the system's long distance and mobility preferences. The ability to read lines of attack is a sensory and intuitive skill that involves detecting finite movement and body language. In Tagalog this is called *geri* and *pakiramdaman.* These skills help the practitioner's techniques become more effective and efficient. Footwork is developed through a series of three controlled sparring drills known as "communication exercises."

"Communication exercises" emulate certain conditions of exchange between combatants to develop and sharpen in students various fighting attributes and skills. They are termed "communication exercises" as practitioners view fighting as a dialectical dialogue between two or more combatants. A unique feature of these exercises are the rhythmic frameworks that in time practitioners learn to quickly recognize and adapt to as they arise in combative encounters. The development of these exercises is partially influenced by Eddie Lastra's background in jazz music. One commonality between the two disciplines is that they are improvisational arts that demand spontaneity.

There are no pre-arranged training forms in Sayas-Lastra Arnis, as these were never a part of classical Arnis training. Indeed, it was, and still is, believed that one's training time is better spent learning how to fight right away than memorizing pre-set movements that may never materialize in combat. And while the late Jorge Lastra did develop and institute a few pre-arranged forms into the system's curriculum, he did so for two "commercial" reason: 1) to help promote the art through Karate tournament forms competitions, and 2) to aid his first

set of students (who all had backgrounds in either Karate or Taekwondo) in relating to Arnis. Such forms are viewed by teachers of this art to be useful in systems that have a lot of complex movements. However, as the Sayas-Lastra Arnis system is rather uncomplicated and to-the-point, the forms have been discarded.

Fighting Strategies

There is only one primary fighting strategy employed in Sayas-Lastra Arnis, and that is the defensive objective of getting off the direct line of attack while simultaneously counterattacking. This strategy is based on the "matador and bull" concept, which is simply going with the path of least resistance and creating room to plot and execute your next move.

Mobility and positioning are the key principles of the art, as open fighting conditions typically demand constant movement to remain out of reach of an opponent's strikes. The other principle employed here being that a moving target is harder to hit than a stationary one. The movements that facilitate this are characteristically angular and circular—although linear and lateral motions are also sometimes used.

In essence, the strategy is to be in a position such that you can strike your opponent without yourself being struck by his weapon. Insofar as this is a long range fighting art, this strategy can be successfully employed through correct footwork and positioning along with the skill of instantly recognizing a strike's in-coming line of attack.

Free-Sparring

As Sayas-Lastra Arnis is a pragmatic fighting art, it utilizes free-sparring with different levels of intensity for practitioners of different levels of skill.

Controlled free-sparring is performed at the novice levels with no safety protection worn, except for optional eye goggles. The sticks used during sparring are usually rattan or light hardwood, but are furnished with padded tips. Thus, only the striking area of the weapon is padded.

Advanced students engage in sparring matches wherein not even the tips of the sticks are padded. To minimize injury, however, the intensity of strikes is controlled as is their placement on critical targets. The exchange is closely monitored by the teacher so the practice does not get out of control.

In addition to these unarmored sparring practices, practitioners of Sayas-Lastra Arnis also occasionally don head guards and hand protectors. As this method enables harder and less-controlled strikes, practitioners develop the skills necessary to be able to function under extreme conditions. However, practitioners refrain from maliciously wailing on one another during such armored sessions, as they recognize the trap of believing sparring with protection is the same as sparring without it.

Training for free-sparring comes by way of the "communication exercises." These exercises are likened to band rehearsal, wherein one can practice their scales, riffs, ideas, and so on, and the free-sparring is likened to the gig and the spotlight which turns to you to take a solo. If students crash and burn on their solos, then they return to the "communication exercises" to find out why, and spend time correcting their errors. It is in this way that practitioners can use the core training of the system to not only develop strong fighting skills but to correct their bad mistakes which could prove fatal in a real encounter.

Tuhon Christopher C. Sayoc, Sr.

26

Sayoc Kali

The art of Sayoc Kali hails from Imus, Cavite and spans five generations. While the system used to maintain twelve weapon categories, today, however, under the direction of Christopher C. Sayoc, the system's focus is almost entirely on the use of knives and their related uses. No doubt, such a focus has made this dynamic art one of the most thorough and well-structured knife-fighting systems in the world.

Training Progressions

There are three main training categories found in the Sayoc system: Kali, Silat, and Bakal. Included in these categories are proper handling of various types of blades, the drawing of blades, vital target discrimination, defenses against and the practice of disarms, blade throwing, and finger-touch methodology (pressure-point manipulation) used in conjunction with knife work. Practitioners are also taught critical injury management.

Blade orientation and respect for the blade is always taught first, thus minimizing over-estimation of edged weaponry self-defense capabilities. Moreover, Sayoc practitioners are always with their blades, and hence, it is a natural evolution to begin a study of how to carry and holster their weapons. Practitioners place an emphasis on being comfortable and familiar with carrying a multitude of blades and weapons on their person at all times.

From the first lesson, the students' minds are exercised, as each person is indoctrinated with the phrase, "knife fighting is a brain game, the smarter you are, the better you will be." Beginners are first introduced to blade handling skills, proper gripping methods, the different components of the blade, and blade selection and targeting. Following this is an introduction to methods of footwork, methods of holstering, rapidly acquiring, and putting blades into play. As students progress further, they are introduced to a number of "vital templates" and associated drills.

The drills are designed to teach body movement and mechanics, footwork, target discrimination, and teach students how to minimize their own potentially dangerous, involuntary reactions. During training, students are presented with a series of probing techniques. These probes are designed to elicit levels of response. As a given level of response is initiated, correction is made and concepts are introduced which allow students to progress in their understanding and application of skills. The progression is very simple. A student will start with blade orientation and will continue through the memory installation process until the basic formulas are installed and become functional. The introduction will continue through to the "thought provocation" method of memory retention and then to the "correct response" method of learning.

The design of this art is feeder (offensively) based, as it is believed that there is diminutive need to learn the defensive

aspects—as these would take an equal amount of time to develop—when one could learn just the offensive aspects to defeat opponents. Thus, the primary training category is Kali, the feeder or armed phase of training. All material in this phase is feeder dominant, thus the entire training, learning, and teaching system is directed toward the development of the attacker.

From this foundation, students are introduced to various "knife tapping" or flow drills that teach a series of transitional movements. From these transitional movements it is possible to derive isolated interpretations and applications of knife fighting techniques. Sayoc Kali knife training is extensive, including over thirty-six basic vital templates for knife work (with an equal amount for the non-dominant hand), with ten transitional flow drills, and an additional number of knife drills taught after the transitional flow drills have been mastered. A system of footwork is taught, as are methods of limb immobilization and lower limb/upper limb destruction, in conjunction with the patterns and flows of knife work.

The next phase of training is Sayoc Silak. As the counterpart of Sayoc Kali, this is the receiver or unarmed defensive phase. Silak provides for the development of empty hand skills, footwork, and body mechanics necessary to trap, lock, position, and disarm the feeder or aggressor's blades. The goals of training in Sayoc Silak are for retention of one's blades, positioning of incoming attacks, preparation for weapons release, and for the loading of one's dominant hand with more blades for various uses. The unique approach to Sayoc Silak is the way in which it is taught and presented. The Silak techniques are incorporated directly into the "transitional flow drills"; hence, the techniques are always practiced against a moving opponent—as opposed to just having a partner stand in a static position with his weapon in a fixed and immobile position to allow the partner to properly execute techniques. Sayoc Silak methodology bridges the gap between Sayoc Kali and Sayoc Bakal, the third phase of training.

Sayoc Bakal complements both the Kali and Silak categories and techniques. Sayoc Bakal is the projectile weapons system and is the key to closing-the-gap between combatants. Projectiles can be released from any position and at any range. Body mechanics are taught to help conceal the angles of trajectory being used. There is specific training to teach how to hold a number of blades in a loaded position for the dominant hand to deliver, and also how to develop quick release grips to avoid having one's hands being trapped or cut by an opponent.

Sayoc Kali uses formulas for development that teach both the feeder and the receiver the proper means to grow in skill and experience. The formulas involve escalating both the feeder's responses, as well as the receiver's responses to achieve maximum potential. Once the feeder knows how to trigger the reflexive response of the receiver, it is possible to ingrain the conditioned response. The conditioned response is the trained reaction to the opponent's/receiver's reflexive response. After exploring the conditioned response, the feeder must learn how to elevate the receiver's response (the opponent's conditioned response), thereby making it more difficult for the feeder to react with a conditioned response. Finally, by trying to keep up with the higher level of the opponent's/receiver's response, practitioners are forced to use the correct response—the most effective conditioned response to a given number of reflexive responses.

There is no set time limit to advancing through the system, as students progress as fast as they can retain and apply information. Once the basic learning formula has been established, it is then demonstrated and explored how and why the system logic exists.

Training Methods

Sayoc Kali does not use general lines of motion or angles of attack—as are found in other Filipino systems—but rather thirty-six basic vital templates of targeting. These templates are specific for different weapons, and purposes, and are presented in such a way as to allow progression for understanding and development. The vital templates of the left hand are not mirror images of the right hand, but independent templates that work in reaction to the right hand, and vice-versa. The left hand vital templates can be applied in combination with the right hand vital templates in a variation of timing entries including a simultaneous attack. The overview would be that the right hand vital template is aggressive and is designed to trigger the receiver's reflexive response and conditioned response. The left hand vital template is designed to react to the receiver's conditioned response. This particular vital template formula leads the receiver to minimize his successful responses.

Twelve transitional flow drills are taught next and serve as a bridge between Sayoc Kali and other systems of combat. The transitional flow drills have steps that are more pronounced and are designed to teach familiarity and skill with using the blade. The Sayoc Kali knife drills, which are separate and different from the transitional flow drills, tend to have more direct movements, using more natural body motion and containing more subtleties for application of the knife, thus economizing power arcs for close quarter work and honing blade edge discipline.

The majority of training in Sayoc Kali is generated from two person or multiple man training drills. Indeed, the philosophy of the art asserts that there is nothing better than a living, breathing, thinking, and responsive training partner to give you back what you give him. The skills and intellect of

your training partners will build and mold your own attributes through the error of your training partner or by way of your own hands. Indeed, every category in the Sayoc system has two person drills, as it is only through physical contact that one can learn how the body will move and react.

Sayoc Kali also uses training forms from the onset of training, but these appear more as skirmishes than dance-like movements. In this art, any movement that is repeated for memory or for practice is considered a form. However, forms are used for nothing other than memory installation and ocular mapping, for the simple reason that the art is energy based and can only be taught and transmitted in that method. The movement of precision cutting and penetrating cannot be exercised effectively without the presence of a moving, thinking, reacting target, and thus pre-arranged solo forms have no place in this system.

Fighting Strategies

Of primary concern to the practitioner of Sayoc Kali is to end an altercation with little or no injury to himself. It is crucial to be able to determine the exact desired extent of the damage applied through the blade—from how to gain lethal entry, to total dismemberment of the body, and, if necessary, to death. This is affected through the implementation of eight primary fighting strategies.

1. Upon closing-the-gap, do not use techniques that attack the incoming limbs. Instead, use opening attacks to penetrate vital targets. This allows for better management of the opponent's reflexive counters and eliminates the teasing of the target that wastes time.

2. Every movement can be applied with single blade, empty

hands, and double blades without any adjustments or modification to the techniques. This ensures that blade to empty hand and empty hand to blade translations will not have a detrimental outcome to the practitioner.

3. From a distance, blades are thrown as projectiles at opponents while closing-the-gap to effectively make the opponents' reactions predictable. These projectiles also serve to keep an opponent off balance, and cause him to move and react in ways to slow him down from reaching his own weapons, or causing him to be in an awkward position as the Sayoc practitioner closes in.

4. Rather than merely relying on speed and power, Sayoc practitioners rely on correct response movements to defeat their opponent's reflexive and conditioned responses. In blade work, the smarter you are, the better you will be. If the techniques you are using are based on speed and power, then anyone with equal attributes stands an equal chance of defeating you.

5. Sayoc Kali utilizes methods of targeting different vital points of the body known as vital templates. This is in contrast to systems that commonly just present a system of angles by which to deliver knife strikes which may or may not have an equivalent degree of effectiveness. The right hand vital templates are designed to counter reflexive and conditioned responses, and the left hand vital templates are designed to react to conditioned and correct responses. A third set of vital templates is used to react to both the right and left hand templates.

6. In multiple opponent encounters, the loader principle comes into play. This strategy positions less experienced close range fighters at a safe range to allow them to use the Sayoc Bakal projectile methods. By doing this, the practitioner is able to maintain a longer range of confrontation, thereby assuring themselves a greater success of walking away unscathed. It is the responsibility of the more skilled and experienced fighters

to close-the-gap and actually engage the opposing combatants. These "buddy system" maneuvers allow practitioners of all skill levels to deal with a number of opponents in group combat.

7. Always position your blades for stealth. One method of addressing this is from the draw or sheathed blade position. The blades are drawn from multiple locations that are easily accessible to the feeders' passing hands. Once the weapons are drawn, the dominant weapon hand applies techniques that obstruct the opponent's view of the blade.

8. Employ various pattern combination techniques, such that an "S" pattern is a combination of three thrusts and a

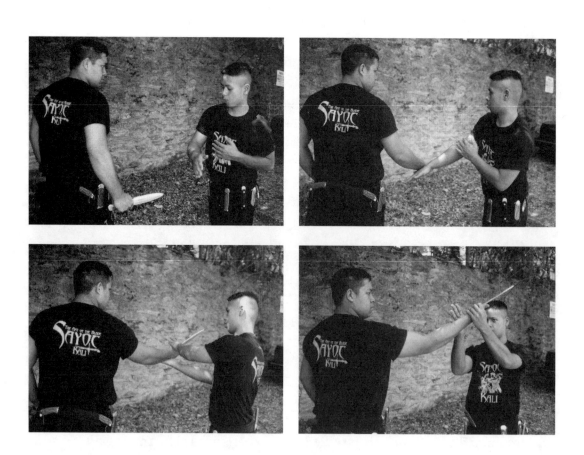

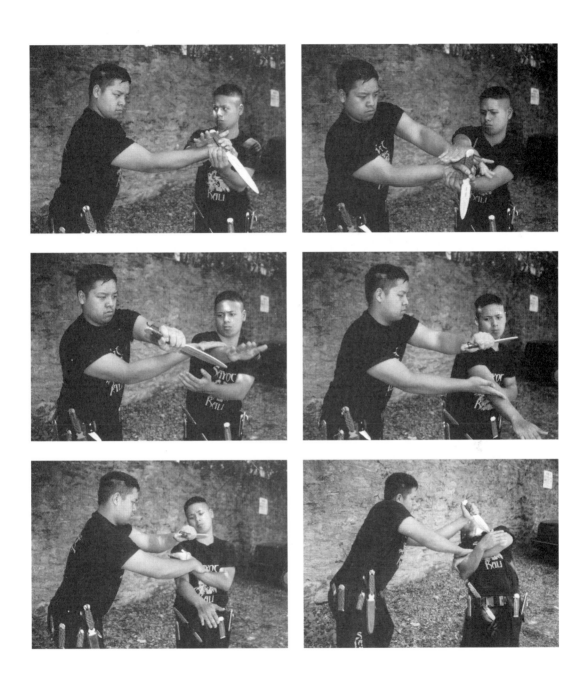

"C" pattern consists of semi-circular cuts. These types of strike combinations are based on timing and multiple redirections. Commonly applied within the vital templates and knife transition flow drills, these techniques prepare the feeder to logically react to the receiver's normal reflexive and conditioned reflexive responses. This particular training formula develops the feeder's proper reflexive responses while under stress from the receiver's lethal target intentions.

Free-Sparring

Sayoc Kali uses a diversity of sparring scenarios to better illustrate to students their weaknesses and strengths. The only way to train for this is to practice steadily and continuously, and seek out correct responses using the formulas as presented. Because the system is energy based, contact is essential. Thus, all training drills have a free-style component to them that is considered free-sparring. Strategies are also taught to force opponents into postures and positions that make them vulnerable to the practitioner's skills.

As students progress, they are encouraged to escalate the amount of pressure applied to their partners in whatever way they can. The partners are also expected to increase their level of response, the objective being to gain control of an opponent during practice. Sayoc Kali varies the contact involved in sparring sessions, depending on what skill is being focused on for that lesson.

While free-sparring, the goal is to gain lethal entry and maintain the lethal entry status until targets are immobilized or one achieves total body dismemberment without himself sustaining injury. Entry skills can be practiced utilizing rules that call for the first lethal blow with a weapon to an opponent "wins." Another can be a full contact match to submission. Some sparring sessions only utilize an impact weapon with the addition of grappling, while others are against multiple opponents.

During free-sparring, or actual combative encounters, the following is kept in mind: Primal or offhand reflexive responses are more likely to occur against aggressive movements which are unfamiliar to you. The left hand vital templates counter the right hand vital templates and there is a third set of vital templates to counter both. Knife fighting is an educated fighter's territory: the more informed you are, the better your chances of survival will be.

Master Rufino Pambuan

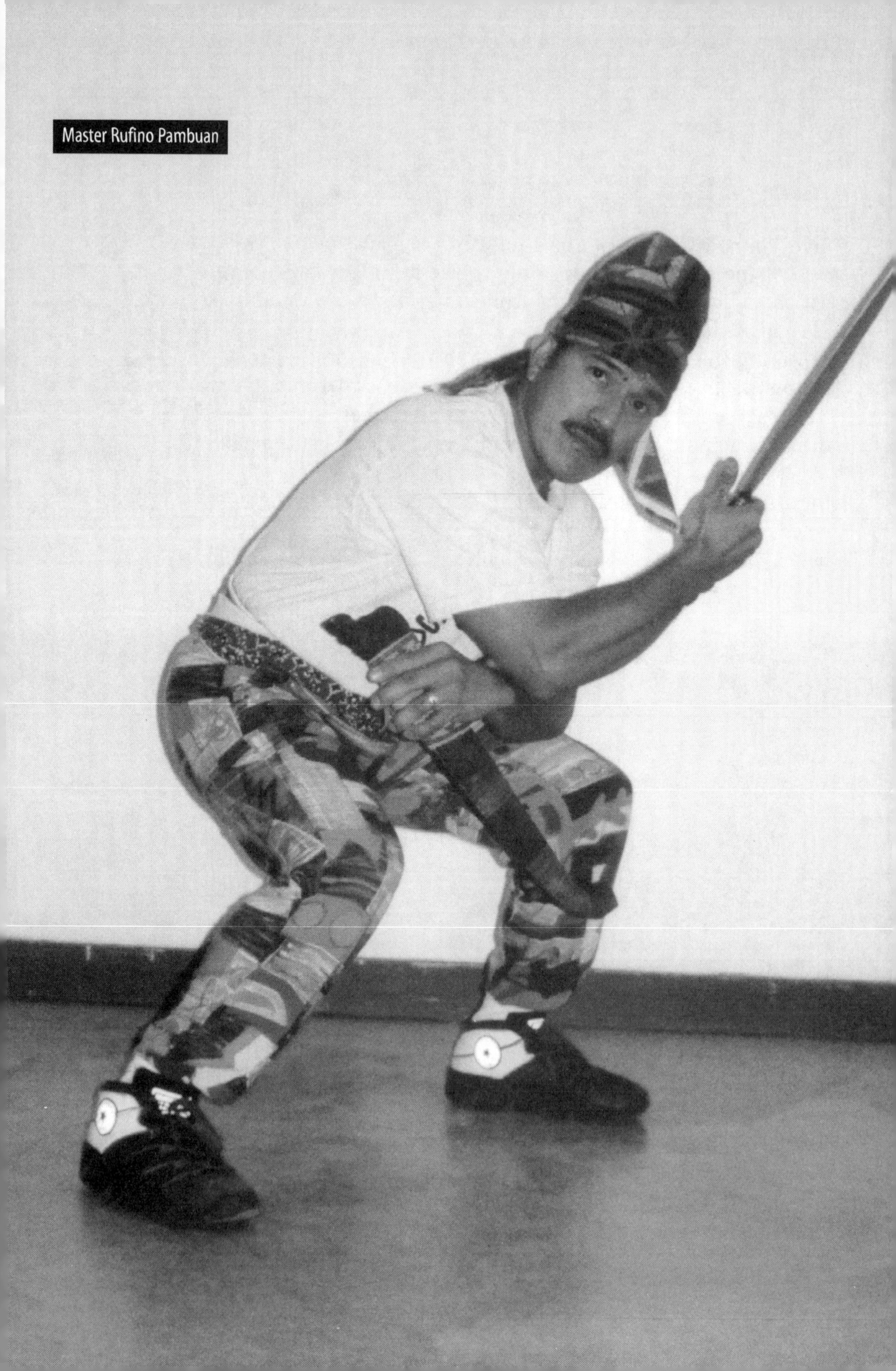

27

Tulisan Caballero Taga-Herada

Tulisan Caballero Taga-Herada is a Filipino fighting art from San Juan, Laguna, Philippines that traces back to Nikolas S. Pambuan and Pelisiano Manabat, the grandparents of Isidro M. Pambuan, the developer of the system. Isidro learned and combined the Manabat Taga-Herada style from his mother's family with the Pambuan Tulisan Caballero style from his father's family, and later added the empty hand arts of Mano-Mano, Buno, and Kuntaw, thus creating a new system whose name reflected those of its predecessors.

Training Progressions

Tulisan Caballero Taga-Herada is a composite system whose training categories include the single stick *(baston)*, single sword *(espada)*, sword and dagger *(espada y daga)*, dagger *(daga)*, horse and bull whips *(latigo)*, and empty hands *(mano-*

275

mano). As a basic progression, practitioners begin with the single stick and end with sword and dagger training.

That the masters and ethics of the Pambuan Arnis Mano-Mano Martial Arst Family are Christian, the art itself employs a Christian-influenced ranking structure based on twelve levels. Such a structure is used as a symbol of man's struggle with himself to become more Christ-like. Each teacher of the art may use a sash, rope, or other indicator to denote rank, wherein there are a total of twelve student ranks (six basic and six advanced) and ten teacher *(guro)* ranks.

The ranks of teacher first level *(guro isa)* through teacher fourth level *(guro apat)* are earned through formal testing examinations. To attain higher ranks a student must be invited into the family association after which they are awarded family ranks. The family ranks run up to and include tenth-degree grandfather teacher *(lolo guro).*

Beginners are indoctrinated into the system with lectures on the art's historical and philosophical underpinnings. Once this has been presented, methods of holding the weapons, warm-up exercises, and footwork are taught. There are eight sets of footwork, including "diamond stepping," "side-stepping," "planting rice steps," and "coconut stepping."

As there are twelve student levels in Tulisan Caballero Taga-Herada, the material leading to the teacher ranks is spread out. The techniques of the single stick are presented from level one onward. At level one, students are taught the basic diagonal, horizontal, and vertical strikes. At level two the system's five angles of attack *(cinco tero)* are taught, followed by the seven angles of attack *(siete pares)* at level three, and the twelve angles of attack *(doce pares)* at level four. Along with learning the proper striking sequences and intended target areas of each strike, basic methods of blocking are taught, including the roof block, side block, umbrella block, cross block, fan block, four wall block, and others. This is followed by

advanced methods of simultaneous blocking and striking, such as the *sunkit* and *taga-herada* methods.

Double stick training is introduced from level four onward. Students are first introduced to the *sinawali* combination weaving exercises, followed by their fighting applications from level five onward.

If students are able to effectively grasp the fundamentals of the art taught in the first seven levels, more advanced weapons and training are introduced at level eight. Such training includes use of the single sword *(espada)*, sword and dagger *(espada y daga)*, empty hand defenses against a knife *(daga)*, and the horse and bull whips *(latigo)*. The whips were introduced into the system by Mike Sayoc, and are important in that they are not only weapons but mechanisms through which students develop precise timing and targeting, body mechanics and hand angling.

During the course of the twelve student levels, but not preset to a specific level, are the skills in *mano-mano* (hand-to-hand fighting), including the arts of Dumog (hand and leg trapping, sweeping, locking, and stick grappling) and Kuntaw (striking and kicking).

For one to be considered for a teacher's rank, they must not only show a physical mastery of all material thus far learned, but also display the deeper specifics of each technique and be able to expound on their underlying theories.

Progression through the ranks is dependent on the individual student and his dedication to the art. Just like anything else, those who study hard and train smart will be rewarded faster then those who do not. And while rank is based on skill, there is also a minimum waiting period of one year for those coming from another Filipino martial art before they are eligible to be considered for a teacher-level rank.

It should also be noted that everyone who trains in the system is expected to give back to the system. As such, everyone

who becomes a teacher is obligated to also teach the art so that it does not perish, as many of the older arts in the Philippines have already done.

Training Methods

There are a number of solo exercises and partner drills utilized in Tulisan Caballero Taga-Herada. Solo training exercises—such as striking a hanging stick and shadow boxing—and partner drills—such *as taga-herada, sinawali,* and *sombrada*—help prepare practitioners for combat by developing their sense of timing, distance, spatial relationship, and mental edge.

Striking and blocking a stick hung from the ceiling at the middle by a rope is a primary method used to develop timing, speed, and agility. This also increases awareness, for once the stick is struck it will swing in unpredictable ways which the practitioner must effectively block or be struck in the head.

While pre-arranged solo forms are viewed as developing in students the bad habit of utilizing only certain fighting combinations, practitioners of this art perform *karenza,* a method of fighting an imaginary opponent that is similar to shadow boxing with a weapon. As novices often find it difficult to improvise their movements, the teacher will first present a basic format and techniques to the students, who then puts them together in their own sequence according to how they feel. *Karenza* is introduced to the students when they want it, and is not a part of the testing requirement.

The primary two-person training drill is known as the "*taga-herada* drill," which finds two partners in a give-and-take exchange. The drill features the umbrella block *(payong)* and the overhead, downward strike *(buhat araw)*. To perform the drill, Partner A executes the overhead strike, which Partner B blocks with the umbrella block from the closed guard. Partner B counters with the overhead strike, which Partner A blocks with the umbrella block from the open guard. The drill then repeats any number of times. At a basic level, the drill is performed while standing still. As students master the movements, the drill progresses to include lateral and circular footwork and changes in the heights of the practitioners.

Another two-person training drill is known as *sumbrada*, meaning shadow or to shadow (or follow) your opponent's movements. This is a counter-for-counter drill wherein partners exchange an equal number of blocks and strikes, set in a series of three movements per side. To perform the drill, Partner A (the attacker) executes a downward, overhead strike *(buhat araw)*, which Partner B (the defender) blocks with an umbrella block *(payong)*. Partner A follows this with a horizontal, forehand strike *(planchada)*, which Partner B blocks with a cross block *(cruzada)* from the open guard position. Partner A follows this with a thrust to the stomach *(sak-sak)*, which Partner B blocks with a cross block *(cruzada)* from the closed guard position. The sequence then repeats on the opposite, with Partner B as attacker and Partner A as defender.

The art of *sinawali* is used to train the double sticks. And while these weaving patterns are common practice in Arnis, many systems only make use of the standard three weaving patterns (i.e., all strikes high, interwoven high and low strikes, and all low strikes). This system, however, chains together the basic three sets of six strikes while also performing counts of four and five strikes inserted at random.

Fighting Strategies

There are several primary fighting strategies utilized in the Tulisan Caballero Taga-Herada system. The preliminary strategy is to avoid conflict. One way of doing this is to never carry two sticks with you while walking or traveling, as this is a key advertisement of your art and someone might ambush you to make a name for themselves. Thus, practitioners only carry one stick with them, so if someone asks about the stick they can say it is a cane or used to keep dogs at bay.

If the practitioner has no option but to fight, he does not initiate the encounter but awaits his opponent's first move. In

this way he forces his opponent to make the first mistake by opening his guard during the strike. From a legal standpoint, having only defended oneself and not initiated the first blow does much to establish innocence.

Tulisan Caballero Taga-Herada is primarily a long range fighting art. As such, practitioners are able to keep their opponent at bay, while employing feinting maneuvers *(enganyo)* to draw reactions and over-commitment. When in long range practitioners are also able to employ finite body angulation to at once be in a position to strike their opponent while being just out of range of his counter strike. Both of these methods allow the practitioner to easily counter or unexpectedly move into medium range with a killing blow *(hataw).*

The key fighting strategy while using all of the above is execution of the *taga-herada* technique. This is a method that either strikes the opponent's on-coming weapon hand from long range or simultaneously parries the weapon hand with the empty hand (or secondary weapon) while at the same time striking the body with the weapon. The strategy here being immediate finishing blow on first strike, rather than blocking then striking or engaging in an elongated exchange of strikes and blocks, which could ultimately lead to the practitioner's doom.

Free-Sparring

Free sparring is a practice long held as an essential constituent to truly mastering the art of Tulisan Caballero Taga-Herada and being able to apply it in real-life combat. Everyone in the art must spar, including beginners, who are introduced to it with light contact "touch sparring." Advanced practitioners are encouraged to engage in full-contact bouts with classmates and practitioners of other styles, and it is left to individual discretion as to how much (if any) body armor one chooses to wear.

Sparring bouts are conducted at the end of every training session, some days featuring harder contact than other says. Regardless of what level one chooses to spar on a daily basis, all practitioners wishing to be considered for a teacher rank must participate in at least one full-contact, unarmored *bahala na* bout—that is, "anything goes."

Further Reading

The following is a comprehensive bibliography of the books on Filipino martial arts proper in various languages. For those interested in reading more information on a particular style, any of these books would be a good place to start.

Anima, N. (1982). *Filipino Martial Arts*. Quezon City, Philippines: Omar Publications.

Bisio, T. (1979). *San Miguel Eskrima Student Handbook*. New York: Author.

Bitanga, D. S. (1984). *The Butterfly Manual*. Kingsport, TN: TCC Publishing.

Bouraca, A. K. & Nardi, T. J. (1994). *Dynamic Kali Knife Defense*. Canoga Park, CA: Koinonia Publications.

Brocka, J. C. (1979). *The Art and Science of Philippine Combat Arnis*. Manila, Philippines: World Union of Martial Arts.

Cabiero, JC. & Vatcher, G. (1996). *The Pure Art of Cabales Serrada ng Escrima*. Fresno, CA: CSE Productions.

Campbell, S., Cagaanan, G., & Umpad, S. (1986). *Balisong: The Lethal Art of Filipino Knife Fighting*. Boulder, CO: Paladin Press.

Cañete, C. (1989). *Doce Pares Association Basic Eskrima, Arnis, Pangolisi*. Cebu City, Philippines: Doce Pares Association.

Cañete, D. (1993). *The Philippines Eskrima, Kali, Arnis.* Cebu City, Philippines: Doce Pares Association.

Davis, A. (1999). *The Legacy of Grandmaster Angel Cabales: Serrada Escrima Explosive Empty Hand Fighting.* Woodland Hills, CA: Koinonia Productions.

Diego, T. & Ricketts, C. (in press). *The Secrets of Kalis Ilustrisimo.* Boston, MA: Tuttle Publishing.

Dowd, S. K. (1978). *Kuntaw: The Ancient Art of Filipino Hand and Foot Fighting.* Stockton, CA: Koinonia Productions.

Dowd, S. K. (1998). *Kuntaw Sayaw-an: The Dancing Techniques.* Woodland Hills, CA: Koinonia Productions.

Fong, L. & Nardi, T. J. (1995). *Modern Escrima: The Explosive Art of Filipino Stick Fighting.* Woodland Hills, CA: Koinonia Productions.

Galang, R. S. (2000). *Complete Sinawali: Filipino Two Stick Fighting.* Boston, MA: Tuttle Publishing.

Imada, J. (1984). *The Balisong Manual.* Los Angeles, CA: Know Now Publications.

Imada, J. (1986). *The Advanced Balisong Manual.* Los Angeles, CA: Know Now Publications.

Inocalla, S. (1988). *Veintenueve Balisong Filipino Knife Fighting.* Canada: Modern Arnis Federation.

Inosanto, D. & Johnson, G. (1980). *The Filipino Martial Arts.* Los Angeles, CA: Know Now Publications.

Jalmaani, A. & Garcia, J. (1976). *Arnis: The Filipino Art of Stick Fighting.* Stockton, CA: Koinonia Publications.

Jalmaani, A. (1979). *Arnis Free Fighting.* Stockton, CA: Koinonia Publications.

Lanada, P. & Mariñas, A. P. (1974). *Arnis de Mano.* Elmhurst, NY: Arnis de Mano.

Laraya, J. (1996). *La Punti Arnis de Abanico Primer.* Ontario, Canada: Author.

Latosa, R. & Newman, W. M. (1979). *Philippine Martial Arts Society Escrima.* Germany: Wu-Shu–Verlag Kernspecht.

Lema, B. L. (1989). *Arnis: Filipino Art of Self-Defense.* Manila, Philippines: Integrated Publishing.

Mahvashi, N. (1996). *La Punti Arnis de Abanico.* San Juan, Philippines: JAFAHA Publications.

Maltese, M. (1999). *Kali: L'arte del Combattimento Totale Filipino.* Roma, Italy: Edizioni Mediterranee.

Mariñas, A. P. (1984). *Arnis Lanada Book 1.* Burbank, CA: Unique Publications.

Mariñas, A. P. (1986). *Pananandata Knife Fighting.* Boulder, CO: Paladin Press.

Mariñas, A. P. (1987). *Pananandata Dalawang Yantok.* San Juan, Philippines: JAFAHA Publications.

Mariñas, A. P. (1988). *Pananandata Yantok at Daga.* Boulder, CO: Paladin Press.

Mariñas, A. P. (1989). *Pananandata Rope Fighting.* Boulder, CO: Paladin Press.

Mariñas, A. P. (2000). *Pananandata Knife Throwing.* Atlanta, GA: Atlanta Cutlery.

Presas, E. A. (1988). *Arnis: Presas Style and Balisong.* Quiapo, Philippines: Author.

Presas, E. A. (1996). *Filipino Armas de Mano: Presas Style.* Quiapo, Philippines: Author.

Presas, E. A. (1996). *Filipino Modern Mano-Mano: Presas Style*. Quiapo, Philippines: Author.

Presas, E. A. (1996). *Filipino Police Combative Techniques*. Metro Manila, Philippines: Author.

Presas, E. A. (1998). *Filipino Knife Fighting*. Quiapo, Philippines: Author.

Presas, R. A. (1974). *Modern Arnis: Philippine Martial Arts*. Manila, Philippines: Modern Arnis.

Presas, R. A. (1980). *The Practical Art of Eskrima*. Manila, Philippines: Modern Arnis.

Presas, R. A. (1983). *Modern Arnis: Filipino Art of Stick Fighting*. Burbank, CA: O'Hara Publications.

Presas, R. A. (1994). *Makabagong Arnis de Mano*. Metro Manila, Philippines: National Book Store, Inc.

Romain, M. (1983). *Escrima Self-Defense*. Boulder, CO: Paladin Press.

Ruperto, E. O. (1996). *The Book of Mastery Movement: Alamid Martial Arts*. Philippines: Author.

Sebastian, R. (1997). *The Turtle: Introducing Kamagong Self Defense*. Tooele, UT: Transcript Bulletin Publishing.

Santos, N. (1977). *Arnis: The Figure Eight System*. Stockton, CA: Koinonia Publications.

Santos, N. (1984). *Arnis: The Up and Down System*. Stockton, CA: Koinonia Publications.

Siebert, G. (1995). *Arnis Escrima Kali*. Berlin, Germany: Verlag Weinmann.

Somera, A. (1998). *The Secrets of Giron Arnis Escrima*. Boston, MA: Tuttle Publishing.

Sulite, E. G. (1986). *Advanced Balisong.* San Juan, Philippines: Socorro Publications.

Sulite, E. G. (1986). *The Secrets of Arnis.* San Juan, Philippines: Socorro Publications.

Sulite, E. G. (1993). *The Masters of Arnis, Kali, and Eskrima.* San Juan, Philippines: Socorro Publications.

Tobosa, R. (1991). *The Systematic Approach to Effective Escrima.* Honolulu, HA: Tobosa Schools of Kali/Escrima.

Tom, W. D. & Tom, W. T. (1983). *Manipulation Manual for the Balisong Knife.* New York, NY: Sunrider Publications.

Westersund, K., Halminen, E. G., Pauwels, P. (1997). *Escrima: Filipino Stickfighting with Links to Ju-Jutsu and Kyusho-Jutso.* Antwerpen-Berchem, Belgium: Authors.

Wiley, M. V. (1994). *Filipino Martial Arts: Cabales Serrada Escrima.* Tokyo, Japan: Tuttle Publishing.

Wiley, M. V. (1997). *Filipino Martial Culture.* Tokyo, Japan: Tuttle Publishing.

Wiley, M. V. (2000). *The Secrets of Cabales Serrada Escrima.* Boston, MA: Tuttle Publishing.

Wiley, M. V. (Ed.). (in press). *Reflections on Arnis.* Boston, MA: Tuttle Publishing.

Yambao, P. (1957). *Mga Karunungan sa Larong Arnis.* Quezon City, Philippines: University of the Philippines.

ABOUT THE AUTHOR

Mark V. Wiley is a researcher and scholar whose involvement in the martial arts spans more than two decades. He has traveled extensively throughout North and South America, Europe, Southeast Asia, and the Far East to train and conduct field research on the martial arts and healing traditions indigenous to those countries.

In addition to being a practitioner of Qigong and Vipassina meditation, Mark holds advanced teaching credentials in the martial arts of Cabales Serrada Escrima, Kalis Ilustrisimo, and Ngo Cho Kun. He has been featured on the covers of the *Journal of Asian Martial Arts, Martial Arts Legends,* and *RAPID Journal* (published in the Philippines), and has been interviewed regarding his research on two radio programs in Mindanao. He has also been nominated to four martial arts halls of fame, but declined induction feeling that such things are too often motivated by politics and monetary gains.

Mark has written several other books, including *The Secrets of Cabales Serrada Escrima* (Tuttle, 2000), *The Secrets of Phoenix-Eye Fist Kung-Fu* (with Cheong Cheng Leong) (Tuttle, 2000), *Martial Arts Talk* (Tuttle, 2000), *Qigong for Health and Well-Being* (with FaXiang Hou) (Journey Editions, 1999), *Filipino Martial Culture* (Tuttle, 1997), and *Filipino Martial Arts: Cabales Serrada Escrima* (Tuttle, 1994). He has written martial arts entries for the *Illustrated Encyclopedia of Body-Mind Disciplines* (Rosen, 1999) and the *Encyclopedia of World Sport* (ABC–CLEO,

1996), and is the author of over 100 articles that have appeared in leading magazines and journals.

Mark has also served as executive martial arts editor for Tuttle Publishing, in their Tokyo and Boston offices, as publishing manager for Multi-Media Books and Unique Publications, as associate publisher of *Martial Arts Illustrated* magazine, editor of *Martial Arts Legends* magazine and *Taipan's Quality of Life,* and as associate editor of the *Journal of Asian Martial Arts.* He is currently group publisher of *247You.com,* associate editor of *FightingArts.com,* and resides in Abingdon, Maryland, with his wife, Jeraldine, and son, Alexander.